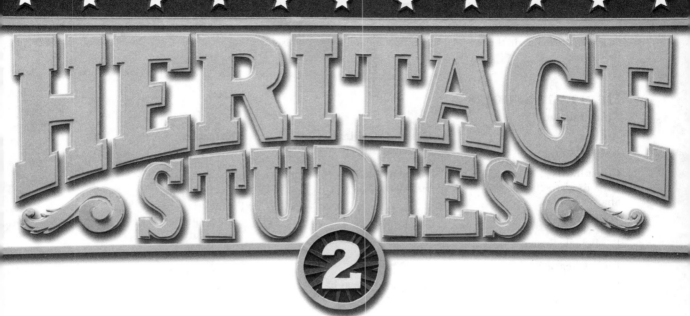

HERITAGE STUDIES 2

Third Edition

bju press®

Greenville, South Carolina

Note

The fact that materials produced by other publishers may be referred to in this volume does not constitute an endorsement of the content or theological position of materials produced by such publishers. Any references and ancillary materials are listed as an aid to the student or the teacher and in an attempt to maintain the accepted academic standards of the publishing industry.

Heritage Studies 2
Third Edition

Author
Eileen Berry

Consultants
Gina Bradstreet
Sharon Fisher
Wendy Harris
Ann Larson
L. Michelle Rosier

Bible Integration
Bryan Smith

Project Editor
Carolyn Cooper

Design Coordinator
Michael Asire

Page Layout
Bonnijean Marley

Cover Design
Elly Kalagayan

Cover Art
Ben Schipper

Cover Photography
Craig Oesterling

Project Coordinator
Kendra Wright Winchester

Illustrators
Paula Cheadle
Zach Franzen
Preston Gravely
Steve Mitchell
Kathy Pflug
Dave Schuppert
Lynda Slattery
Del Thompson

Permissions
Sylvia Gass
Kathleen Thompson
Carrie Walker

Photograph credits appear on pages 223–24.

© 2014 BJU Press
Greenville, South Carolina 29609
First Edition © 1981 BJU Press
Second Edition © 1996 BJU Press

Printed in the United States of America
All rights reserved

ISBN 978-1-60682-471-9

15 14 13 12 11 10 9 8 7 6

Contents

What Is Heritage Studies?

The BJU Press Heritage Studies materials are a presentation of social studies that integrates civics, culture, economics, geography, and history. Beginning with the framework of God's redemptive plan, *Heritage Studies 2* includes an age-appropriate study of civics, government, and geography. It then covers United States history from Native Americans to the founding of the independent nation, all from a Christian worldview. Scripture verses, eye-catching artwork, maps, graphs, photos, and quick-check questions enhance learning.

History

History is the study of the past. I study history to understand what has happened and how God has used it. The past helps me understand the world today.

Geography and Culture

Geography is the study of places on the earth around us. **Culture** is the way of life of a group of people. I study geography to find my way around God's world. I study culture to learn how people live all over the world.

Economics

Economics is the study of the way we use goods and money. I study economics to learn the best ways to use God's gifts.

Citizenship

Citizenship is the study of my community, my state, and my country. I study citizenship to learn how God wants me to help my leaders and my land.

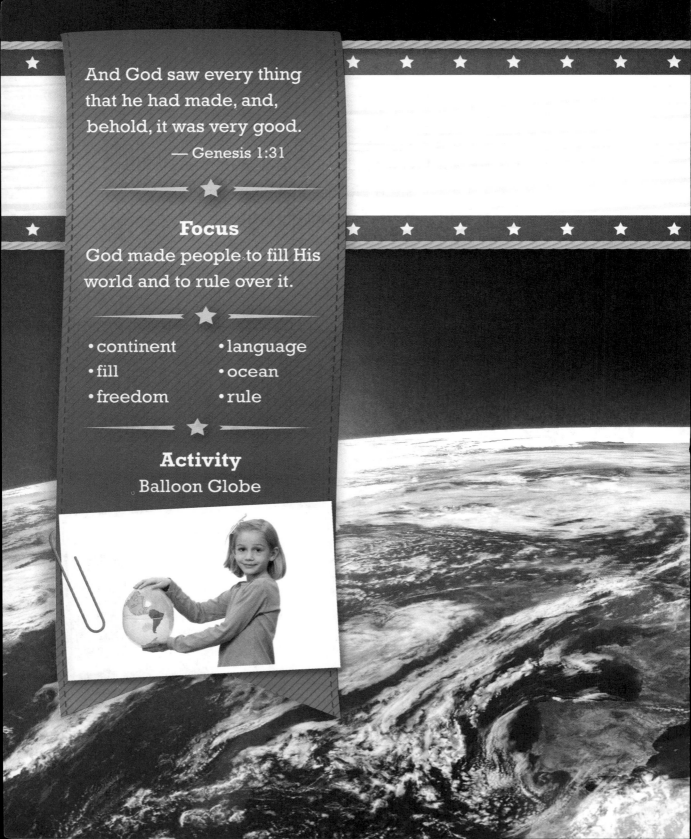

And God saw every thing that he had made, and, behold, it was very good.

— Genesis 1:31

Focus

God made people to fill His world and to rule over it.

- continent
- fill
- freedom
- language
- ocean
- rule

Activity

Balloon Globe

God So Loved the World

Creation

The world began with God. God made the world out of nothing. He made light. He made the earth, the sky, and the sea. He made the sun, the moon, and the stars. He made plants, trees, and animals. Last of all, God made people. God created everything just by speaking.

God's world was perfect and beautiful. There was no sin in it. There was no pain, sadness, or death in the world. God looked at everything He had made. He called it very good.

God had made a man and a woman. The man was Adam, and the woman was Eve. God made them in His image. He made them like Himself in certain ways.

God put Adam and Eve in the Garden of Eden. God told them to have children. He wanted them to **fill** the earth with people who loved Him. He told them to **rule** over His perfect world.

What job did God give Adam and Eve?

9

Sin

God gave Adam and Eve **freedom**. "You may eat freely of every tree," He said. He also gave them a rule. "But there is one tree you may not eat from. If you eat its fruit, you will die."

Adam and Eve had freedom, but they also had a rule to obey. One day they chose to break God's rule. They chose to sin. Pain, sadness, and death came into the world. God's world was no longer perfect.

The Savior

God always keeps His word. Adam and Eve would die for their sin. They would suffer pain and sadness. But God also had a perfect plan. One day He would send a perfect Savior, Jesus Christ.

Jesus would die for the sins of the world. He would be raised to life again. Jesus would save people from their sin. He would take away the power of death. He would rule as Adam should have. He would fill the earth with people who love and obey God.

John 3:16

God so loved the world that He gave His only Son.

What was God's perfect plan?

People Fill the World

After Adam and Eve sinned, they had to leave the Garden of Eden. They had children. Their children had children. People kept sinning. People became so wicked that God sent a flood to destroy them. Only Noah and his family lived through it.

After the Flood, God planned for people to spread out and fill the world. But years went by, and people did not obey. One day some people decided to build a huge tower. They wanted to stay together and be strong. But God caused people to speak many different **languages**. They had a hard time talking to each other. The work stopped.

The tower of Babel was never finished.

13

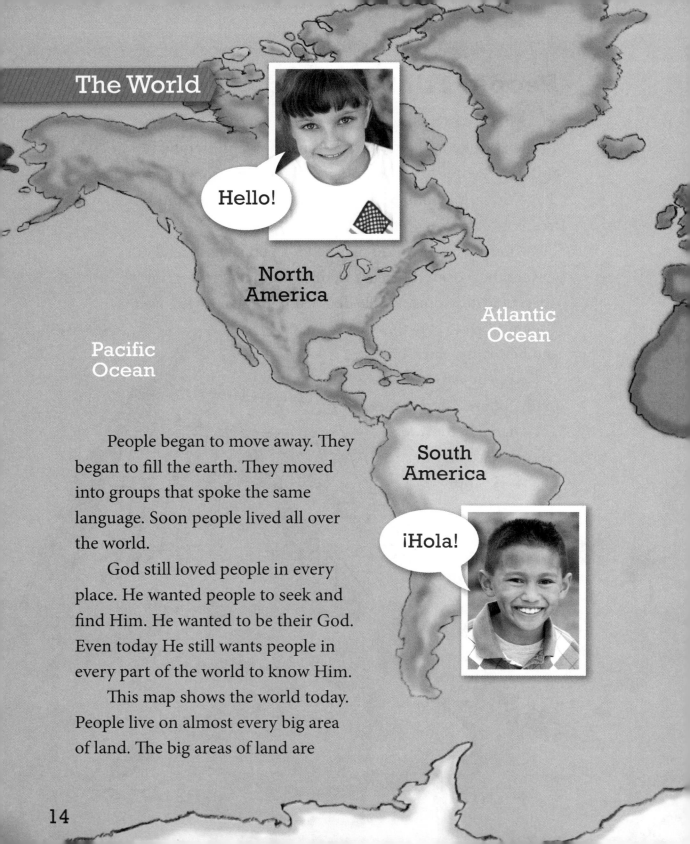

North
America

Atlantic
Ocean

Pacific
Ocean

South
America

People began to move away. They began to fill the earth. They moved into groups that spoke the same language. Soon people lived all over the world.

God still loved people in every place. He wanted people to seek and find Him. He wanted to be their God. Even today He still wants people in every part of the world to know Him.

This map shows the world today. People live on almost every big area of land. The big areas of land are

Arctic Ocean

Ciao!

Ni hao!

Europe

Asia

G'day!

Africa

Jambo!

Indian Ocean

Australia

continents, and the large bodies of water are **oceans**. There are seven continents and four oceans.

People still speak many different languages today. This map shows children from different parts of the world. Each one has a different way of saying hello.

What continent do you live on?

Antarctica

How Many People?

Look at the **bar graph**. It shows how many people live on each continent. The colors of the bars are the same as the colors on the map of the world. Which continent has the most people? Which has the fewest people?

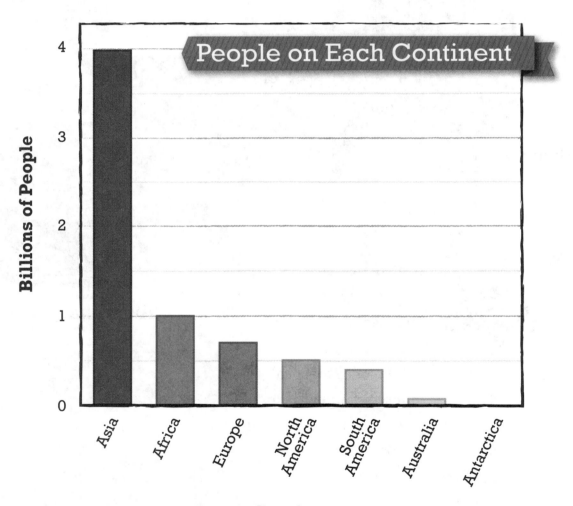

People on Each Continent

Billions of People

Continents

Asia · Africa · Europe · North America · South America · Australia · Antarctica

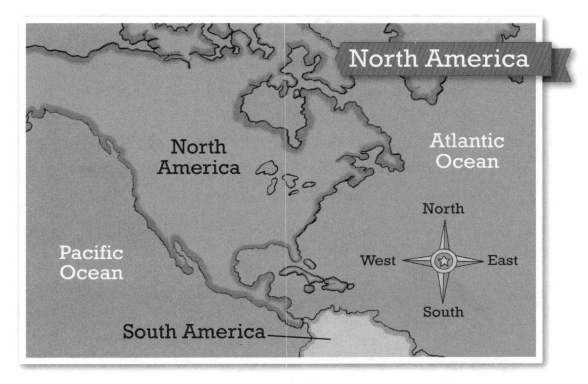

Places on a Map

The **compass rose** shows directions on a map. On this map it is shaped like a cross. The four points show north, east, south, and west. The compass rose helps us find places on a map.

This map shows the continent of North America. We can use the compass rose to find the continent to the south. The compass rose also shows us which oceans are west and east of North America.

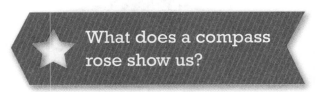

What does a compass rose show us?

Places on a Globe

A **globe** is round like the earth. Globes show directions too. North is at the top of a globe. South is at the bottom. West is to the left, and east is to the right.

The top of the globe is called the **North Pole**. The bottom of the globe is called the **South Pole**. The **equator** is the line around the widest part of the globe.

North Pole

Equator

South Pole

North

West — East

South

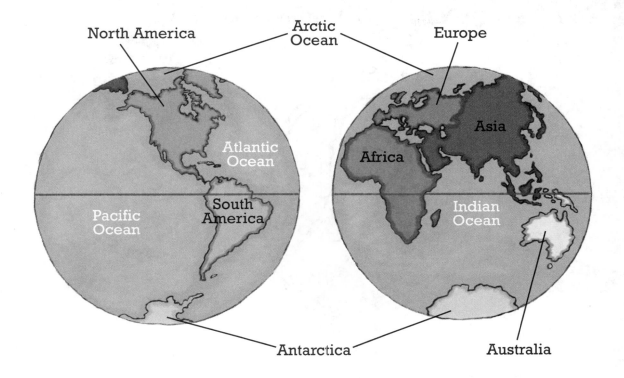

The North Pole, the South Pole, and the equator cannot be seen on the earth. But we can see them on a globe. We use them to help us find places on the earth.

Some continents are north of the equator. Some are south of it. The equator runs right through some of the continents.

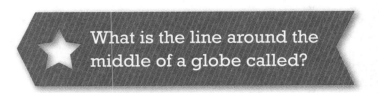

What is the line around the middle of a globe called?

Adoniram and Ann Judson

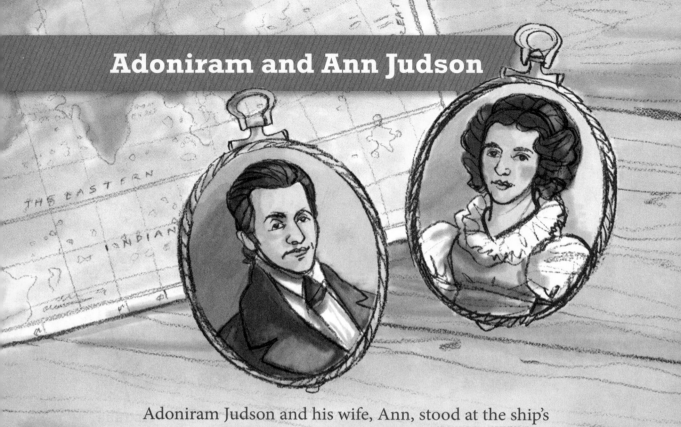

Adoniram Judson and his wife, Ann, stood at the ship's rail looking out to sea. They watched the waves rise, dip low, and gather again. Their home in North America was now far away. Each wave rolled them closer to the continent of Asia. They planned to be missionaries in India.

But when they got to India, they found out they could not stay. They decided to go to the country of Burma instead.

In Burma the Judsons met people who had never heard of Jesus. They began to learn the language of the people. They built a house out of bamboo and grass. "Come into the house and hear about Jesus," they told the Burmese people. After many years, a few people believed.

Mr. Judson began to put the Bible into the Burmese language. War came to Burma before he finished. Burmese soldiers kept Mr. Judson in prison for many months. "You must be a spy," they said.

Mrs. Judson visited her husband in prison and cared for him. All through this time, God kept the Burmese Bible safe. When the war was over, Mr. Judson finished his work. Now the Burmese people had the Bible in their own language. Another part of the world would now be filled with people who love God.

Who kept the Burmese Bible safe during the war?

By love serve one another.
— Galatians 5:13

Focus
God made people to live, work, and serve others in their communities.

- community
- laws
- mayor
- volunteer

Activity
Working Together

Community Life

The First Community

Adam and Eve had a son named Cain. Cain moved to the land of Nod. He lived apart from God. Cain, his wife, and his children began a **community**. A community is a place where people live and work together. People do many kinds of work in a community.

The people in Cain's community worked hard to fill the earth and to rule over the place where they lived. One man took care of animals. Another man learned to play music well. Another made tools out of iron. But something was not right. Cain's community was doing what God made people to do. But they were serving themselves. They were not serving God.

What is a community?

Types of Communities

People today live in many different kinds of communities. An **urban** community is in a city. In urban communities people live close together. Taxis, buses, and trains roar. Subways whiz underground. Many people walk along the sidewalks. People often work in tall office buildings and stores.

A **suburb** is a community near a city but away from the busy part. Suburbs are made up mostly of houses. Families play and have cookouts in their yards. Many people in suburbs drive to work.

In a suburb houses have bigger yards.

In an urban community homes are often close to the street.

A **rural** community is far from a city. We sometimes call a rural community "the country." Houses are far apart. Many houses have large areas of open land or forest around them. Often people in rural communities are farmers and ranchers. They work on their own land. They grow foods like corn, wheat, and beans, or they raise animals. Towns in rural areas are much smaller than cities.

Many communities today are like Cain's community. People work together to do what God made people to do. But they do not want to serve God. They want to serve themselves.

In a rural community there may be large areas of open land where animals can live.

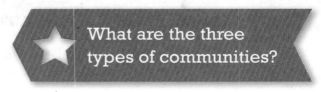

What are the three types of communities?

In Your Neighborhood

You and the people who live and work around you are a **neighborhood**. Communities are made up of many neighborhoods. Sometimes your neighbors become your good friends.

Your neighborhood might have mostly houses. It might also have a school, some churches, and a grocery store. It might have a park where you can swing, walk your dog, or play soccer.

Do you have a favorite place in your neighborhood?

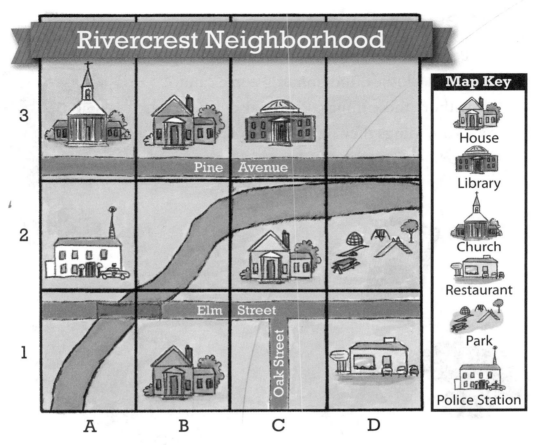

Rivercrest Neighborhood

Pine Avenue

Elm Street

Oak Street

Map Key

House
Library
Church
Restaurant
Park
Police Station

A   B   C   D

1   2   3

Here is a map of a neighborhood. It has a grid. A **map grid** is made up of lines that form squares. The letters and the numbers on the grid help you find places.

Put a letter and a number together. Place your finger on the letter. Slide it up the map until it lines up with the number. You have found a square on the grid. What do you see in that square?

Now find a place on the map. Slide your finger to its letter. Then slide your finger to its number. Which square is it in?

Needs and Wants

People in communities have needs. People need food, clothes, and homes. People cannot live without these things. People also have wants. Wants are things they would like to have. A new toy, a cell phone, and a bigger van are wants. People do not need these things to live.

Families work so they can buy things they need or want. The money your family earns is its **income**. Sometimes families have to save money until they have enough to buy something. A **bank** is a safe place to keep money. Most communities have a bank.

At a bank people save money for things they need and want.

Workers in communities sell things people need and want. Some people make or sell **goods**. Food, cars, and computers are goods. A person who makes, grows, or sells goods is a **producer**. If you buy or use the goods, you are a **consumer**.

Producers

Consumers

Some people offer **services**. A service is something that helps people. A pastor teaches God's Word in a church. A music teacher teaches a skill. A dentist cleans and fixes teeth. A daycare worker cares for children. Consumers pay for these services.

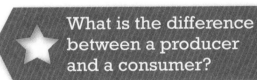

What is the difference between a producer and a consumer?

Volunteers

Some people do not get paid for their services. They give them for free. Some firefighters are **volunteers**. They serve their community for free by keeping it safe during fires.

You can be a volunteer in your community too. Maybe there is a neighbor who needs your help. Maybe you could visit an older person who lives alone. There may be other children in your community who need to hear about Jesus and His love. God may use you to make your community the kind of place He wants it to be.

People in your community need help.

People in your community need Jesus.

What is a volunteer?

Firefighters are easy to reach if there is a fire in your community. Call 9-1-1 on the phone. Tell what you know about the fire. Firefighters will come from the nearest fire station as quickly as they can.

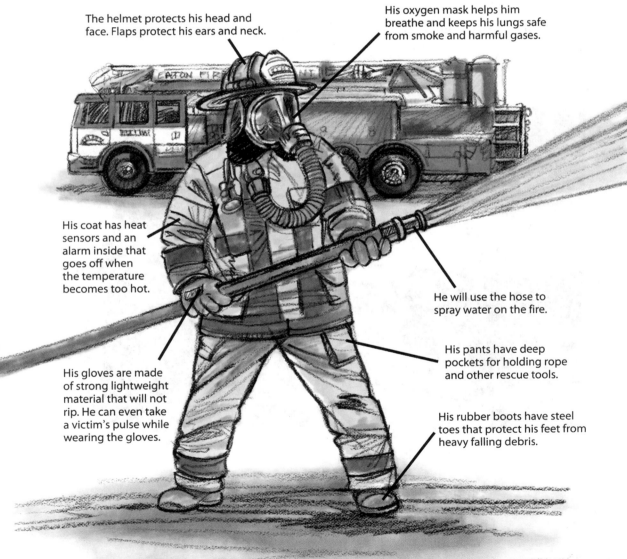

The helmet protects his head and face. Flaps protect his ears and neck.

His oxygen mask helps him breathe and keeps his lungs safe from smoke and harmful gases.

His coat has heat sensors and an alarm inside that goes off when the temperature becomes too hot.

He will use the hose to spray water on the fire.

His gloves are made of strong lightweight material that will not rip. He can even take a victim's pulse while wearing the gloves.

His pants have deep pockets for holding rope and other rescue tools.

His rubber boots have steel toes that protect his feet from heavy falling debris.

33

Community Laws

God wants people to obey **laws**. He gave people the first laws. Just like Adam and Eve, we have freedom. But we use our freedom well only when we choose to obey God's laws.

Your community also has laws. Laws are rules people follow when they live together. Laws help make a community safe. They help solve problems. They keep a community running smoothly. You help your community when you obey its laws.

Traffic laws help keep people safe when crossing streets.

Taxes help pay these city workers to clear streets after a storm.

People in a community work together to decide laws. They choose leaders. These leaders make the laws the community needs.

People in a community pay **taxes**. Community leaders use tax money to pay for goods and services the community needs. Taxes help pay police officers, park rangers, and other city workers.

The leader of your city or town is the **mayor**. The mayor helps make laws for your community. The mayor works to make the community a good, safe place.

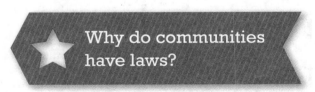

Why do communities have laws?

Rudy Giuliani

A Community Leader

Rudy Giuliani was the mayor of New York City in 2001. Mr. Giuliani had an important job. On September 11, the city was attacked. The two World Trade Center towers fell. Thousands of people were killed. Many others were hurt. People no longer felt safe. People were sad and very scared.

Rudy Giuliani

Mr. Giuliani did not panic. He worked hard. He helped police and firefighters get their jobs done. He made wise choices. Slowly the city was cleaned up. People began to feel safe again. The people of New York will always remember Mr. Giuliani as a strong leader in a hard time.

Communities Change

As people fill the earth and rule over their places in the world, changes come. Your community has not always been the way it is now. You may live in a suburb that was once a rural community. Communities change over time. New buildings are built. Sometimes old ones are torn down. More and more people might move to a community. Or people might move away. Communities can grow bigger or smaller.

God put you in your community for a reason. You can serve your community in a special way. You might even be able to help change it. Look for ways to make your community a better place to live.

Here are two photos of a place in New York City. How has this place changed over time?

 What are some ways communities change?

37

He that ruleth over men must be just, ruling in the fear of God.

— 2 Samuel 23:3

★

Focus

God has given citizens and their governments responsibilities to each other.

★

- citizen
- government
- just
- nation
- responsibility
- right

★

Activity

Voting

Liberty and Justice for All

3

God's Kind of Leader

Cain's community was not the only kind of community long ago. In another community much later, God gave the people a leader who loved Him. The people were God's chosen people, the Israelites. Their leader was David.

David learned that a good leader is a person who does what is **just**. He tries to be fair and right. A good leader also loves God and seeks to please Him. David had a heart to seek God. He helped the Israelites remember to trust and love God. David led his people to overthrow many of God's enemies.

David knew he did not always do what was just. He did not always obey God. Sometimes he failed to be a good leader.

But David knew things would be different one day. One day God would give the whole world a different kind of Leader. That Leader would always do right and always obey God. That Leader did come. His name was Jesus. One day He will come back. Until He does, God wants all leaders everywhere to rule as Jesus will rule. He wants all leaders to rule justly and to obey Him.

> What makes a leader good?

Your Three Governments

Just as God gave people leaders long ago, He gives them to us today. People everywhere have leaders.

Are you a **citizen** of the United States of America? A citizen is a person who belongs to a certain place. As a United States citizen, you are part of three groups. You are part of a community. You are part of a state. You are also part of a **nation**, or country. God has placed leaders in each of these groups. Your leaders are called your **government**.

Your community has a local government. Your mayor is the leader of your local government. Your community might also have a **council**. A council is a group of leaders that work together. Your city council decides what would be best for your community. It is part of your local government.

Your state has its own government too. A **governor** is the leader of a state government. Your governor lives and works in the same city as your other state leaders. This city is your state capital. If you visit your state capital, you will see the capitol building where your state's leaders meet.

You belong to a community, a state, and a nation.

The United States has its own national government. The **president** is the most important leader of the national government. He lives and works in the nation's capital city. The capital of the United States is the city of Washington, DC. The president works with a group of lawmakers called **Congress**.

This chart shows your three governments.

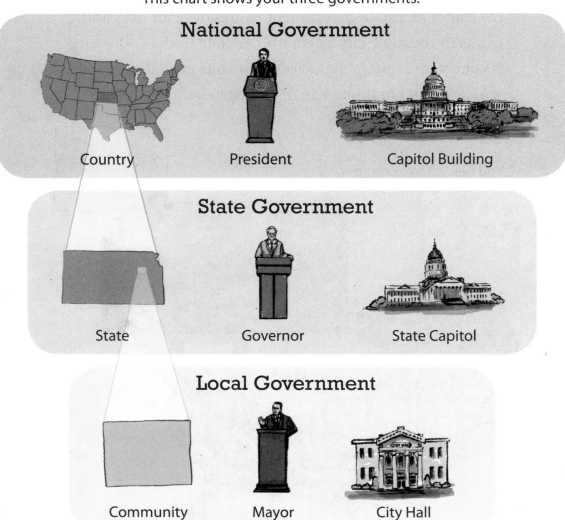

National Government

Country   President   Capitol Building

State Government

State   Governor   State Capitol

Local Government

Community   Mayor   City Hall

What Governments Do

People living in groups need rules and laws. Your family needs rules. Families have rules about bedtime or keeping rooms neat. Schools need rules. Your classroom has rules about when to talk and when to listen. Citizens have laws too.

Government leaders make laws for citizens. You have learned that your community has laws. Your local government makes laws for your community. Your state government makes laws for your state. Your national government makes laws for your country.

Local government workers repair community streets.

State government workers make sure citizens obey state laws.

Citizens also have **rights**. A right is something you are free to do. Citizens of the United States all have certain rights. They are free to talk or write about anything. They are free to live and work where they choose. They can choose what they believe.

Government leaders protect the rights of citizens. Governments must be careful to be just. All people should be treated fairly. But some people use freedom to hurt others or to dishonor God. God does not want people to use rights in this way. Good laws protect the rights that God wants people to have.

Governments also provide services. The government uses tax money to pay workers in these service jobs.

National government workers sort and carry mail.

Name two things governments do.

Choosing Leaders

How do we get our leaders? In the United States, citizens **vote** for their leaders. Choosing leaders by voting is called an **election**. Each citizen votes for someone he thinks will do a good job.

Voting is a right of American citizens. People can vote at age eighteen. Citizens who vote wisely find out all they can about those who want to be leaders. They learn about each leader's beliefs and goals. They listen to speeches. They read articles. They try to make the best choices they can.

Romans 13:1–2

God is the one who chooses leaders. He wants us to obey them.

On Election Day people go to voting places. They use a **ballot** to vote. A ballot is a list of all the people who want to be elected.

People vote for leaders. But God is the one who really chooses leaders. He chooses who will win elections. You may not agree with everything your leaders decide. But the leaders you have are the leaders God wants you to have right now. He wants you to obey your leaders.

How do citizens of the United States choose their leaders?

Ronald Reagan

Ronald Reagan was the fortieth president of the United States. He was elected in 1980. He served his country four years. Then he was elected again in 1984.

People voted for Reagan because he was a strong leader. He helped protect our nation's safety. He made our armed forces strong. He helped other nations gain freedom for their people.

President Reagan cared how the American people used money. He made sure people were not paying too much tax. Businesses were then able to offer more people jobs.

President Reagan was a leader who made many wise choices. He faithfully served the citizens of the United States.

Responsibilities of a Citizen

Citizens have a **responsibility** to obey laws. A responsibility is something you should do. When citizens obey laws, they keep the place they live safe. They help keep order in their community, state, and country.

Citizens have other responsibilities too. They should use their freedom wisely. They should take care of the people, places, and things around them. They should remember that other citizens have the same rights they do.

What is this driver's responsibility?

When citizens do not meet their responsibilities, problems come up. Sometimes citizens break laws. People are hurt or harm is done. There are **consequences** for breaking laws. Consequences are what happens because of something we do.

Often people who break laws have to go to court. Local, state, and national governments have courts. **Judges** in courts use laws to settle problems. They decide consequences for breaking laws. They decide what is just and right. A judge might decide that a citizen must pay a fine. Sometimes a judge decides that a citizen must go to jail.

What responsibilities do citizens have?

National Symbols

Our nation has special **symbols**. A national symbol reminds citizens of an important person or idea. Our flag is a symbol of our freedom. You have learned to say the Pledge of Allegiance to the flag. You place your hand over your heart and look at the flag. These actions show that you love and respect your country. The pledge reminds us of the important ideas of freedom and justice. It reminds all citizens to be true to the United States.

Our national bird is the bald eagle. The bald eagle is strong and brave and free. We want our country to be this way too.

Our national **anthem** is a symbol of our country. An anthem is a special song. "The Star-Spangled Banner" is our national anthem. People have fought in wars so our country can be free. This song reminds us to be brave and true like those people.

We can show our love for our country by praying for it. We can ask God to bless our nation. We can ask Him to help our leaders be just. Some songs about our country are written as prayers.

What does our national anthem remind us of?

Landmarks

Some symbols remind us of presidents who led our country well. The Washington Monument is one of our national symbols. It reminds us of our first president, George Washington. Washington led our nation through its first war. He was known for being truthful and wise.

Thomas Jefferson was our third president. Jefferson was skilled with his pen. His writings are still famous today. The Jefferson Memorial was built in honor of him. Many of his quotes can be read on its walls.

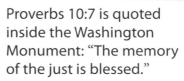

Proverbs 10:7 is quoted inside the Washington Monument: "The memory of the just is blessed."

Inside the Jefferson Memorial are the words "God is just."

Psalm 19:9 is inscribed on the walls of the Lincoln Memorial.

The Lincoln Memorial reminds us of Abraham Lincoln. He was our sixteenth president. Lincoln led our nation during a sad time. Two parts of the country were at war with each other. Lincoln wanted peace and freedom for all Americans.

All three of these symbols are **landmarks**. They are important buildings to see. They can all be found in Washington, DC.

What three landmarks remind us of presidents?

Citizens from Many Places

Were you born in the United States? Then that is how you became a United States citizen. People who were not born in the United States can choose to become citizens too. The United States has citizens from many places in the world.

An **ancestor** is a person in your family who lived long ago. Some of your ancestors might have come to America from another country. They chose to become United States citizens. People who move to a new country are called **immigrants**. Immigrants to America have brought different ways of life with them.

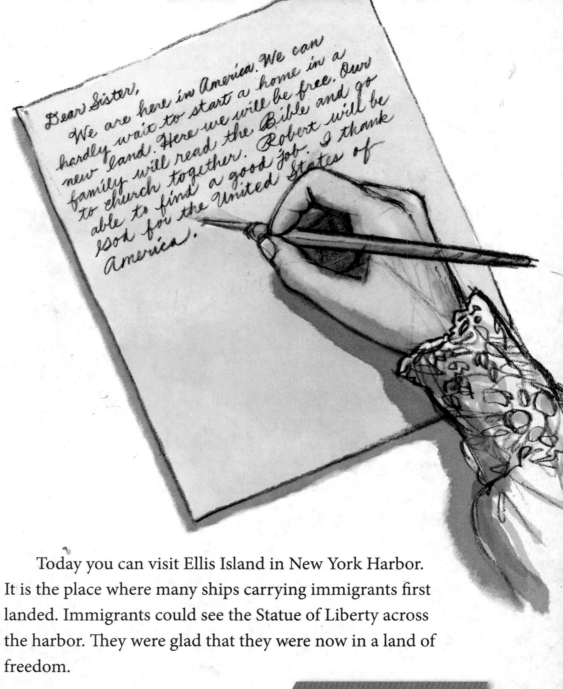

Dear Sister,

We are here in America. We can hardly wait to start a home in a new land. Here we will be free. Our family will read the Bible and go to church together. Robert will be able to find a good job. I thank God for the United States of America.

Today you can visit Ellis Island in New York Harbor. It is the place where many ships carrying immigrants first landed. Immigrants could see the Statue of Liberty across the harbor. They were glad that they were now in a land of freedom.

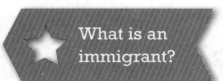

What is an immigrant?

> The earth is full of thy riches.
> — Psalm 104:24b

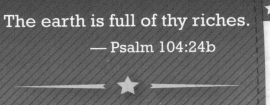

Focus

God has blessed our country with different resources, landforms, and bodies of water.

- climate
- natural resource
- landform
- region

Activity

Travel Map

Land That I Love

Regions

God has always wanted people to fill the earth. He wanted them to live in every part of the world. He knew that people in different places would have different lives.

In the United States, some people live on the coast near an ocean. Some people live on the rich farmland in the middle of our country. Some people live in rainy places and some in dry places. Different parts of the country are called **regions**.

These fishermen live near the ocean.

This rancher lives in a dry region.

Natural Resources

Regions have different **natural resources**. A natural resource is something in nature that God gives people to use. Water, soil, trees, and rocks are natural resources. What natural resources are found where you live?

God wants people to rule over the earth. He wants us to build cities and roads, plant crops, and make beautiful bridges. But God also wants us to love others. We should rule the earth in a way that helps others. We can plant new trees in place of those we have used. We can keep our water and air clean. By taking good care of our resources, we show love for those living around us.

A greenhouse in California uses the sun's light and heat to help plants grow.

A wind farm in Kansas helps people use the power of the wind.

What is a natural resource?

Climates

God planned for regions to have many types of weather. The usual weather a region has in each season is called its **climate**. Some regions have hot, dry climates. Some regions get more rain. Your climate might be warm in summer and cold in winter. Do you live in the northern part of our country? You might get more snow than someone farther south.

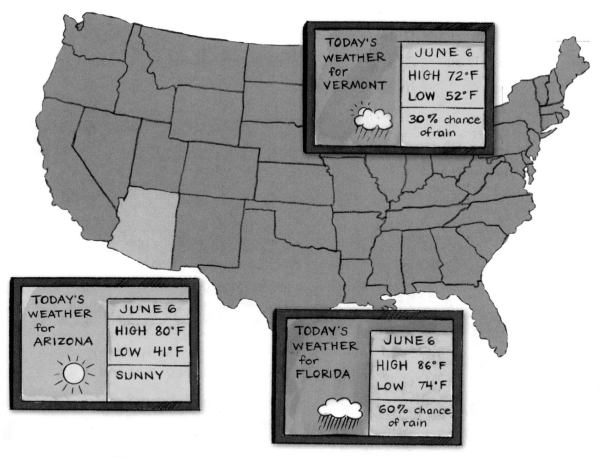

Different regions of the United States have different climates.

People in different regions do different kinds of work. A region's natural resources and climate might be good for a certain job. What jobs would people who live near an ocean have? They might fish, work on a ship, or run a ferry. They might work in a **factory** that cans fish. A factory is a place where people produce goods. What job would someone who lives in a forest region have? He might study plants or cut down trees for lumber and firewood.

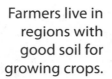

Farmers live in regions with good soil for growing crops.

People in cold climates can do jobs like this in the winter.

What is the climate like in the region where you live?

63

Landforms

Different regions have different **landforms**. A landform is a certain shape of land on the earth. There are many different types of landforms in the United States. Some of them formed as a result of the Flood. The pictures show several landforms. Which ones have you seen before?

hills

mountains and valley

plain

peninsula

island

A mountain is the highest landform. Some mountains are too high for trees to grow at the top. A hill is not as high as a mountain. A plain is a flat area of land. Plains are often covered with grass or crops. A valley is low land between mountains or hills. An island is land with water all around it. A **peninsula** is land with water on three sides.

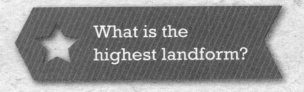

What is the highest landform?

65

Bodies of Water

Bodies of water also come in different shapes and sizes. A river might be long and narrow. A lake might be wide and round. A gulf is water that is partly surrounded by land. Our country has several kinds of bodies of water.

river

lake

gulf

Reading a Landform Map

Your state is in a certain region of the United States. Different regions of our country have different landforms and bodies of water. Look at the landform map. Find your state. What landforms and bodies of water are near your state?

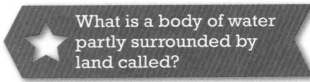

What is a body of water partly surrounded by land called?

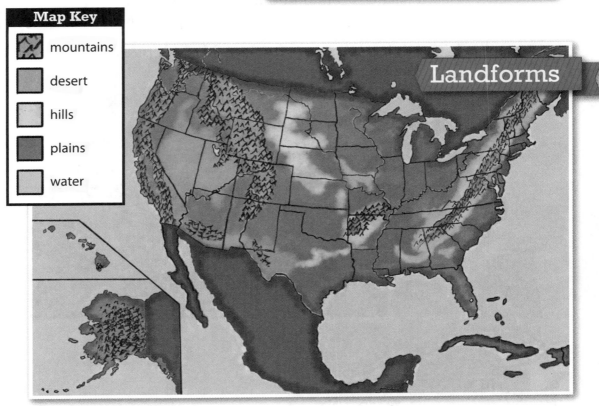

Map Key

- mountains
- desert
- hills
- plains
- water

Landforms

Crater Lake National Park

Crater Lake National Park is in the state of Oregon. Look at the photos. What landforms and bodies of water do you see?

Crater Lake is the deepest lake in the United States. It is more than 1,900 feet deep at its deepest part. It was formed by a volcano sometime after the Flood.

The lake is surrounded by mountains. A large island called Wizard Island is found in the lake. It is made up of ash and rock from the volcano. Phantom Ship Island is a smaller island. It has tall spires that look like a ship's masts.

Oregon

The climate in the park is cool in summer and very cold in winter. Heavy snow falls around the lake during the winter months. Sometimes the snow can be fifteen feet deep.

The park has rich natural resources of soil, water, and forests. Crater Lake National Park is a beautiful place to visit. Every year people visit in summer to camp, fish, hike, and bike in the park.

Crater Lake with a
view of Wizard Island

Phantom Ship Island

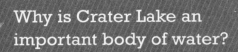

Why is Crater Lake an important body of water?

America's Neighbors

Canada

Canada is the United States' neighbor to the north. It is one of the largest countries in the world. Although it is larger than the United States, fewer people live there. Canada is filled with mountains, forests, plains, and lakes. Many islands lie off the northern coast.

Northern Canada has a very cold climate. It receives more snow and ice than the south. In some regions, the ground stays frozen all the time. The southern part of Canada has milder winters and warm summers. The west coast receives heavy rainfall.

Canada has important natural resources such as forests, water, oil, and natural gas. Many people visit Canada to fish, hunt, and see its wildlife.

Mexico

Mexico is our neighbor to the south. Mexico has high mountains and low plains along the coast. A high, flat area of land called a plateau is in the center of Mexico.

Mexico's regions have different climates. The northwestern region is mostly hot and dry. The mountain regions can be very cold. Sometimes they get snow. Another region of Mexico is a warm, wet area called a rainforest.

Some of Mexico's natural resources are silver, copper, and gold. It is also a top producer of corn, sugar cane, and avocados. Many people visit Mexico to see its colorful culture and history.

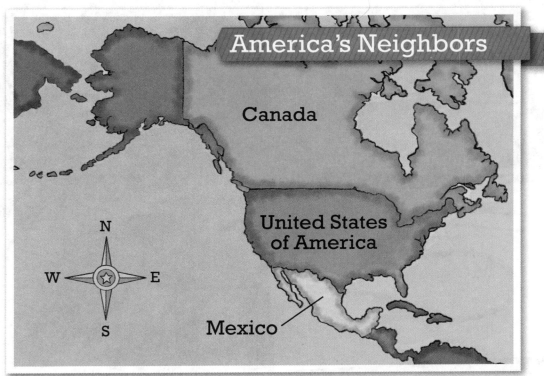

America's Neighbors

Canada

United States of America

Mexico

N
W · E
S

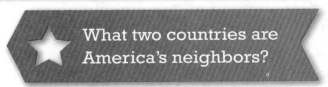

What two countries are America's neighbors?

71

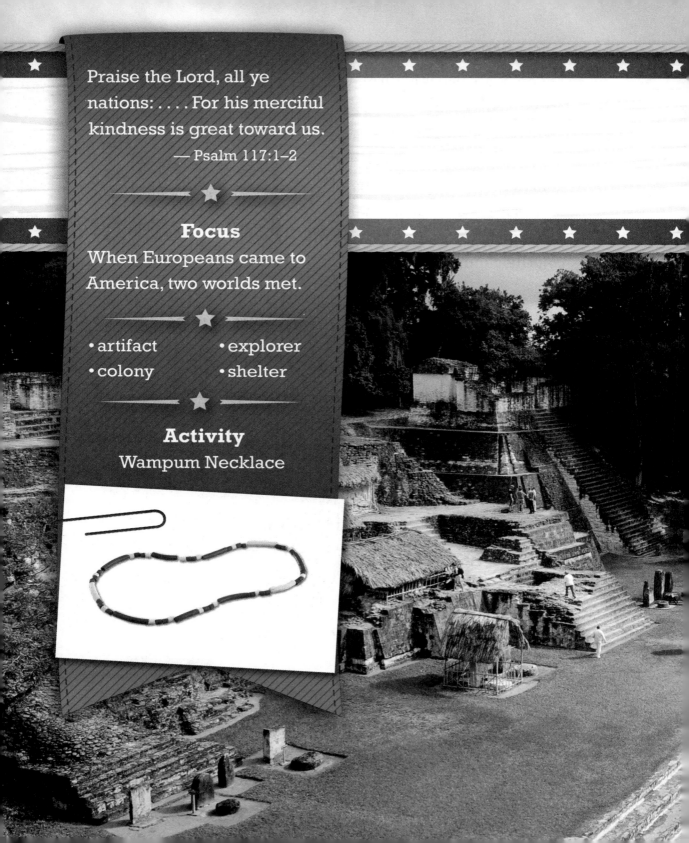

> Praise the Lord, all ye nations: . . . . For his merciful kindness is great toward us.
> — Psalm 117:1–2

Focus

When Europeans came to America, two worlds met.

- artifact
- colony
- explorer
- shelter

Activity

Wampum Necklace

Exploring Our Past

5

The First Americans

Long before many of your ancestors came to America, people lived here. They roamed the mountains and hills. They fished in the lakes and rivers. They hunted on the plains. Where did these first Americans come from?

You have read about the tower that was never finished. God caused people to speak different languages. They stopped their work on the tower of Babel. They scattered around the world.

Some of those people made their way to North America. They were the first Americans.

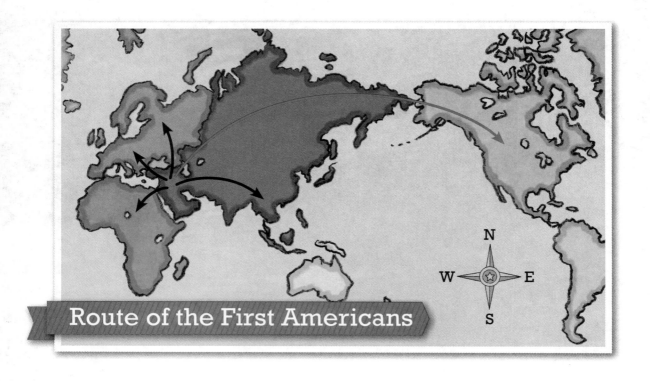

Route of the First Americans

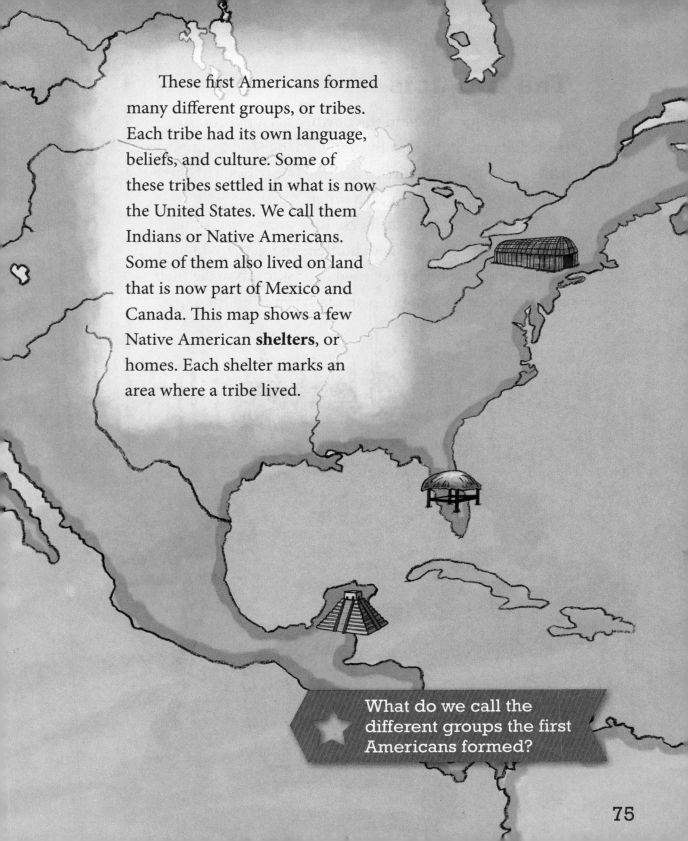

These first Americans formed many different groups, or tribes. Each tribe had its own language, beliefs, and culture. Some of these tribes settled in what is now the United States. We call them Indians or Native Americans. Some of them also lived on land that is now part of Mexico and Canada. This map shows a few Native American **shelters**, or homes. Each shelter marks an area where a tribe lived.

What do we call the different groups the first Americans formed?

The Iroquois

The Iroquois lived in the northeastern part of the United States. Some also lived in Canada. The Iroquois were made up of five Indian tribes. These five tribes had agreed to live in peace and help each other.

The Iroquois were farmers. They grew corn, squash, and beans. They also fished, hunted, and gathered nuts and berries in the woods. They used deer skins to make their clothes. In early spring they made syrup from the sap of maple trees.

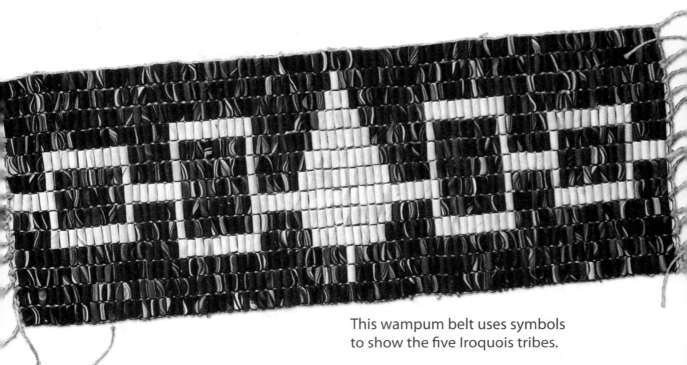

This wampum belt uses symbols to show the five Iroquois tribes.

The Iroquois made small beads called **wampum** from shells. They traded wampum for things they needed. Stringing wampum on a belt was a way to tell a story or send a message.

The Iroquois lived in longhouses. A **longhouse** was a long, narrow home. The Iroquois built a frame of wooden poles. They covered the poles with flat pieces of bark. As many as twenty families might live together in a longhouse. But all the families had the same ancestor.

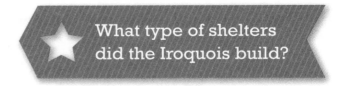

What type of shelters did the Iroquois build?

The Calusa

The Calusa lived in the southeastern United States where Florida is today. They made their homes on the coast. They were not farmers like the Iroquois. They fished and hunted for their food.

The Calusa have been called "the Shell People." They are known for gathering and using shells. They built cities on huge mounds of shells and earth. Their cities had walls and ramps. They had waterways for canoes. Some of their shell mounds can still be seen today.

The Calusa left many things behind that tell us about their lives. Objects left behind by people long ago are called **artifacts**. Artifacts like tools and jewelry tell us the Calusa were skilled. Knives and arrows tell us they were hunters and warriors. Most of these objects were made of shells.

The Mayas

The Mayas were a large group of Indians. They lived in Mexico and other countries to the south. They built beautiful cities of stone. The **ruins** of some of these cities can still be seen in Mexico today. A ruin is what is left of a building from long ago.

The Mayas had many skills. They wrote down their language. They invented the idea of zero. They learned to tell time by the stars and made a calendar. They even made chocolate from beans.

Like other Native Americans, the Mayas did not worship God. They believed that spirits lived in animals, rain, and plants. They built huge temples for these spirits. They thought they had to please the spirits or bad things would happen.

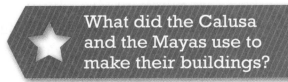

What did the Calusa and the Mayas use to make their buildings?

Explorers from Europe

Hundreds of years after the first Americans settled in North America, people from Europe began to come. Some were trying to find a faster way to sail to Asia. Others had heard about land to the west. They wanted to see it. A few wanted to tell North Americans about God and the Bible. Most hoped to find gold, spices, and other riches. We call these people **explorers**.

Leif Ericson

Leif Ericson loved to explore. His people, the Vikings, were brave sailors and had sturdy ships. They had already come from Iceland to Greenland. But Ericson heard about land farther west and wanted to go see it for himself.

Ericson set out from Greenland around the year 1000. He landed on the coast of Canada in Newfoundland. Later Vikings formed a settlement there. Ericson may have been the first European to set foot in North America.

Christopher Columbus

Christopher Columbus was born in Italy in the 1400s. When he grew up, he lived in Portugal. He sold books, made maps, and worked as a sailor. He too wanted to sail west. He wanted to find a faster way to reach Asia. Asia was the place to find gold, silks, and spices for trading.

The king and queen of Spain agreed to help Columbus. They gave him ships, and Columbus hired sailors. In 1492 he set off on his voyage. He sailed for weeks without reaching land. His sailors began to worry. They were almost out of supplies.

Then one day the sailors spotted land. They had made it all the way across the Atlantic Ocean. Columbus thought he had reached Asia. But really he had landed on one of the islands off the coast of Florida. Today we call these islands the Bahamas.

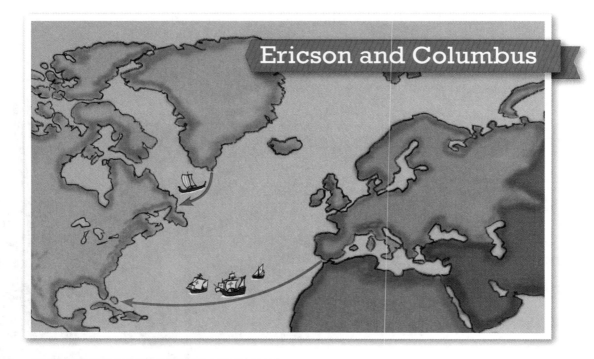

Ericson and Columbus

What part of North America did Columbus reach?

Columbus had once visited Iceland. There he might have learned of the voyage Ericson had taken 500 years before.

Ponce de León's Route

Juan Ponce de León

People in Europe soon learned that Columbus had not reached Asia. He had reached a land they had not known about. They began to call this land the New World.

Other Europeans also came to the New World. One of these was Juan Ponce de León from Spain. He had sailed with Columbus on one of his voyages. Ponce de León settled on one of the islands Columbus had found. One day he heard about a wonderful spring that would make old people young again. He sailed northwest, hoping to find this spring. He never found it, but he found land. He did not know that the land he found was part of a continent. He named the land Florida.

Other Explorers

More and more Europeans came to the New World. They came from Spain, England, and France. The French were interested in trade. They wanted to find a waterway through the continent to Asia. But later they became interested in trading with the Native Americans. They explored rivers and set up trading posts. They traded goods for animal furs.

Native Americans and Europeans had very different cultures. They did not understand one another. Native Americans did not always welcome Europeans. Many Europeans did not treat the Native Americans well. This problem would become bigger and bigger as time went on.

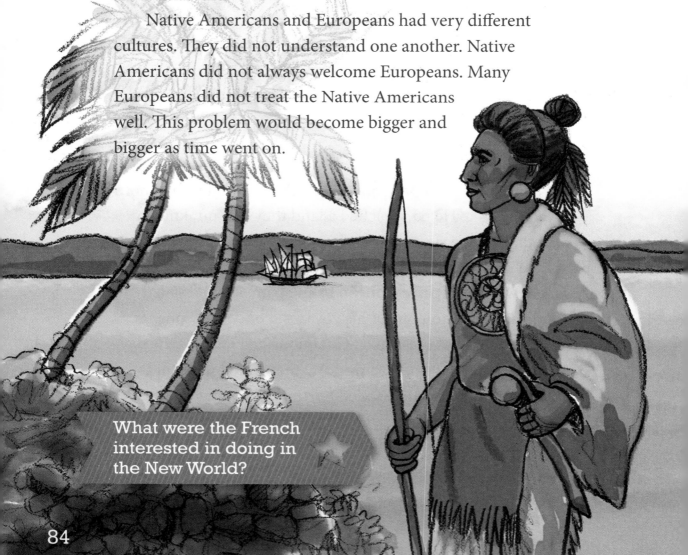

What were the French interested in doing in the New World?

A Colony in the New World

In 1607 three small ships sailed into a bay along the east coast of America. The ships carried men from England. The men had come to start a **colony** in the New World. A colony is formed when people from one country settle in another. A colony usually keeps close ties to its home country.

The Englishmen named their colony Jamestown after King James of England. They called the place they settled Fort James. Soon they realized the Native Americans who lived nearby were not always friendly. The men built a tall log fence around the fort.

Life was not easy in Jamestown. Many of the men would not work. Many became sick. Many even died.

One of the men, John Smith, wanted to get along with the Indians. They knew good places to hunt and fish. They knew which plants would grow well. Perhaps they could help the men of Jamestown.

One day some men from the Powhatan tribe captured Smith and brought him to their chief. Chief Powhatan's young daughter, Pocahontas, became Smith's friend. Soon the chief let Smith return to Jamestown. Pocahontas visited the fort often. She brought food. But the English and the Powhatan still did not trust each other. They sometimes fought and even killed each other.

Life at Jamestown got better. John Smith became the leader of the men. He made all the men work. The men learned to grow crops. They built new houses. Women came to Jamestown and helped form families. King James let Jamestown have its own government.

John Smith returned to England. Later Pocahontas was kidnapped by an English sea captain. During her stay with the English, a pastor told her of Jesus Christ. She became a Christian. She married an Englishman named John Rolfe.

What problems made life at Jamestown hard?

Slaves in the New World

Jamestown was the first English colony to last in the New World. More and more people from England came to live there. They needed more help with their crops. Some Europeans and Africans came to Jamestown to be servants. They worked for food, clothes, and land. After a few years of work, they could be free.

Before long, the Europeans began making African people **slaves**. A slave had to work for the rest of his life. He could never be free. Slavery would be a long, sad part of American life for many years to come.

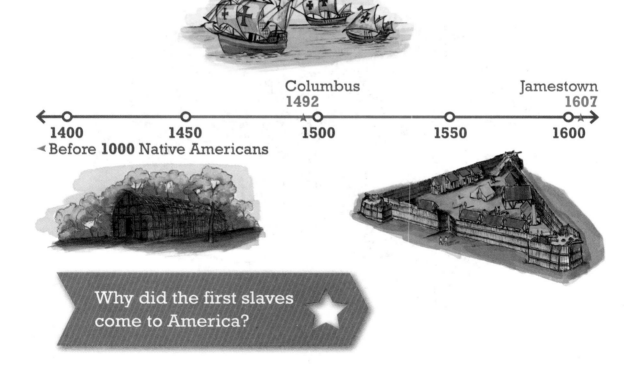

Columbus
1492

Jamestown
1607

← 1400   1450   1500   1550   1600 →
◄ Before **1000** Native Americans

Why did the first slaves come to America?

Robert Hunt

Robert Hunt was a preacher who came to Jamestown in 1607. Hunt believed God had a job for him to do in the New World. He wanted to tell the Indians about Jesus Christ.

Hunt became the pastor of the men at Jamestown. Every day he called them together to pray. Every Sunday he preached God's Word. He helped the men settle problems. He comforted them when they were afraid. He did not complain, even when a fire in the fort burned up his books. He trusted God to do what was best.

Robert Hunt died during his first year in Jamestown. But the men never forgot his brave faith in God.

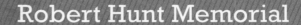

Robert Hunt Memorial

"We all loved him for his exceeding goodness."

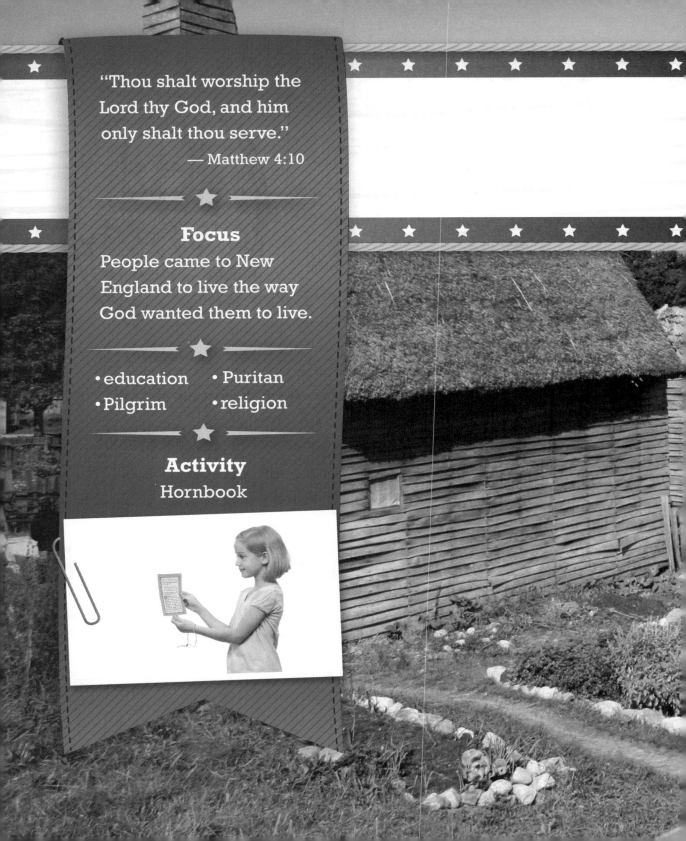

"Thou shalt worship the Lord thy God, and him only shalt thou serve."
— Matthew 4:10

★

Focus
People came to New England to live the way God wanted them to live.

★

- education
- Pilgrim
- Puritan
- religion

★

Activity
Hornbook

The New England Colonies

6

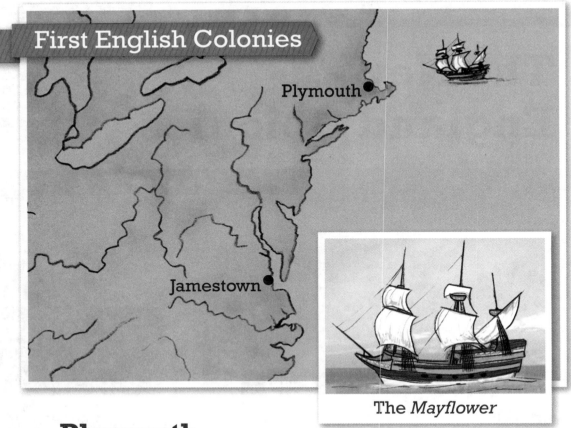

First English Colonies

Plymouth

Jamestown

The *Mayflower*

Plymouth

On a cold November day, an English ship reached the New World. The *Mayflower* had been blown and tossed at sea. The sailors planned to land just north of Jamestown. But storms carried the ship much farther north. God had brought the *Mayflower* to the northeast coast of America.

Many of the people on the *Mayflower* were a group called the **Pilgrims**. The Pilgrims had lived in England. The king of England would not let them worship God in their own church. His law said everyone must go to the Church of England.

The Pilgrims did not believe the Church of England was right. They wanted to obey God and the Bible. The Pilgrims decided to leave England and the church. They came to America in 1620.

The Pilgrims were thankful to be in America. Now they could worship God in the right way. They had come to America because of their **religion**. Religion is a person's belief about where he came from, how to worship, and how to live.

Before leaving the ship, the Pilgrims signed an agreement. This agreement was called the Mayflower Compact. It said that they needed laws in the New World. They agreed to make just laws.

What freedom did the Pilgrims want to have in the New World?

Squanto taught the Pilgrims how to plant corn, squash, and beans.

The Pilgrims' colony was called Plymouth. Life in Plymouth was very hard that first winter. The Pilgrims did not have enough to eat. Many became sick, and many died.

But God sent an Indian named Squanto to help the Pilgrims. Squanto had learned to speak English. Squanto showed the Pilgrims how to grow crops. He taught them how to catch fish and eels. He helped them trade with the Indians. The Pilgrims worked hard, and soon they had what they needed.

Americans still celebrate
Thanksgiving each year.

Plymouth also had a good leader. The Pilgrims elected
William Bradford to be their governor. At the end of
the first year, Bradford led a special feast. The Pilgrims
invited the Indians to the feast. They thanked God for His
goodness. We call this feast the first Thanksgiving.

For many years Bradford led the colony wisely. He
helped the Pilgrims remember to trust God.

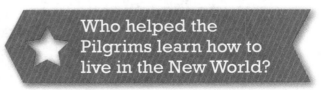

Who helped the
Pilgrims learn how to
live in the New World?

Massachusetts Bay

Ten years after the Pilgrims arrived, another group from England came to America. This group also came because of their religion. They were called **Puritans**.

Like the Pilgrims, the Puritans did not agree with the Church of England. But they did not leave the church. They wanted to stay in the church and help it change.

Over time, some Puritans saw that they needed to leave. The church was not changing. The government found ways to hurt them and their families. A group of Puritans decided to leave England and go to the New World.

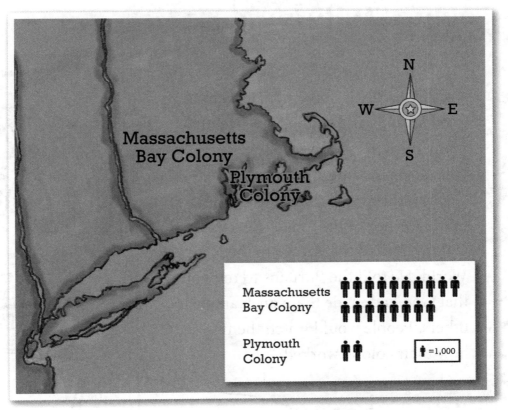

Massachusetts Bay was north of Plymouth.

The Puritans settled in a colony called Massachusetts Bay. Massachusetts Bay became a much bigger colony than Plymouth. In the first ten years, thousands of people came to the colony. After a while, Plymouth became part of the Massachusetts Bay Colony.

Many of the people who came to Massachusetts were Puritans. The government leaders and the pastors were Puritans. They made laws that said no one should speak out against the Bible. They wanted their colony to obey God.

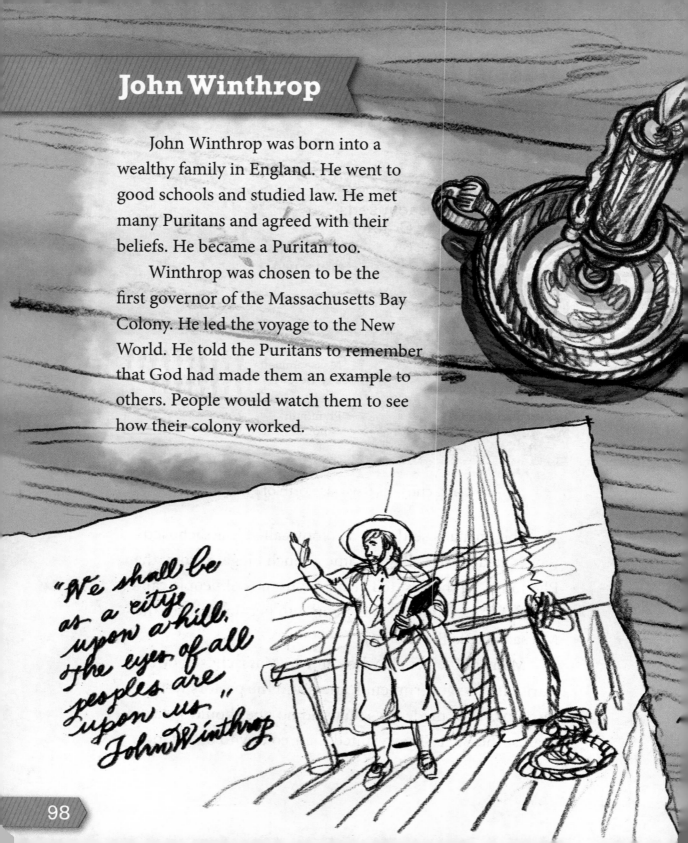

John Winthrop

John Winthrop was born into a wealthy family in England. He went to good schools and studied law. He met many Puritans and agreed with their beliefs. He became a Puritan too.

Winthrop was chosen to be the first governor of the Massachusetts Bay Colony. He led the voyage to the New World. He told the Puritans to remember that God had made them an example to others. People would watch them to see how their colony worked.

"We shall be as a city upon a hill. The eyes of all peoples are upon us."
John Winthrop

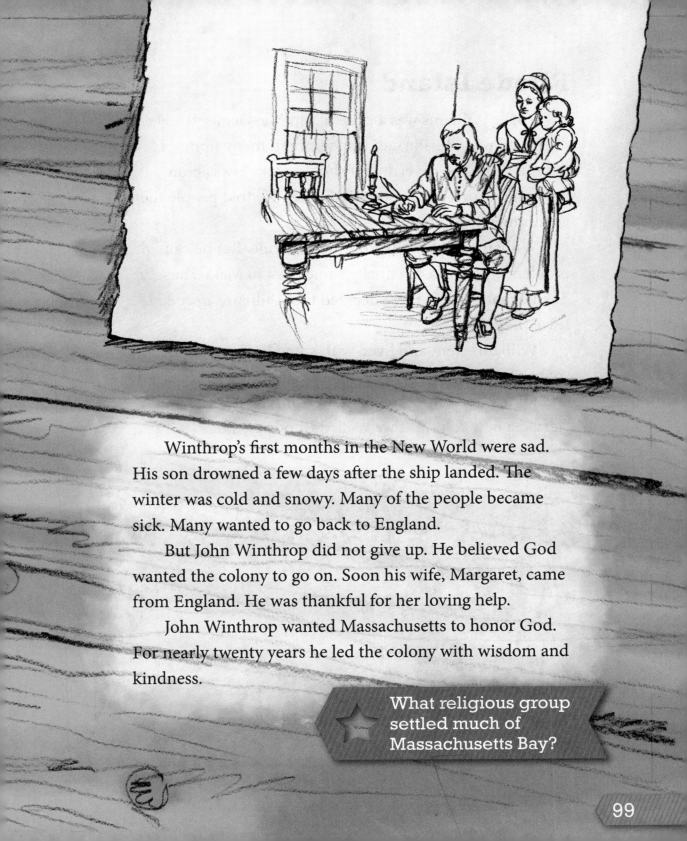

Winthrop's first months in the New World were sad. His son drowned a few days after the ship landed. The winter was cold and snowy. Many of the people became sick. Many wanted to go back to England.

But John Winthrop did not give up. He believed God wanted the colony to go on. Soon his wife, Margaret, came from England. He was thankful for her loving help.

John Winthrop wanted Massachusetts to honor God. For nearly twenty years he led the colony with wisdom and kindness.

What religious group settled much of Massachusetts Bay?

Rhode Island

Roger Williams was a preacher in Massachusetts. He disagreed with the Puritan leaders about many things. He did not think the government should make laws about religion. He preached about his beliefs. He told people the government was wrong.

Williams went to Plymouth for a while. But he caused problems there too. He finally came back to Massachusetts. The Puritan leaders there decided that Williams needed to leave the colony.

Williams went and lived with some Indians to the south. After a while, some people from his old church came and joined him. They bought land from the Indians and started a new colony. It was called Rhode Island.

Connecticut and New Hampshire

Massachusetts became crowded. More and more people, or **colonists**, were coming to live there. There was no more room to build farms. There were fewer places to hunt. Finally, some people decided to move away.

One group of colonists moved west. Their leader was a pastor named Thomas Hooker. They made a plan for their government. They called their colony Connecticut.

Other groups moved north. They formed several towns. For many years these towns were part of Massachusetts. Then they became a separate colony called New Hampshire.

The New England Colonies

This map shows the four colonies on the northeast coast of America. Most of the Europeans who first settled this area were from England. We call these colonies the New England colonies.

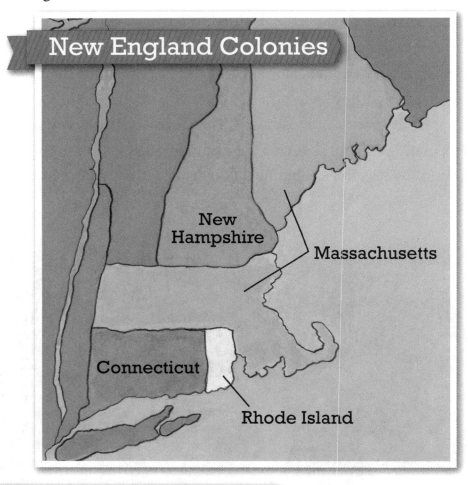

New England Colonies

New Hampshire

Massachusetts

Connecticut

Rhode Island

What were the four New England colonies?

Life in New England

Many people in the New England colonies lived on farms. They raised cattle, pigs, chickens, and crops for their own families.

But the land in New England was not very good for farming. It had rocky soil and hills. Many people used other natural resources to make a living. Fish and whales swam in the waters. Plenty of trees grew in the forests. Colonists caught and sold the fish. They hunted whales and used their oil and bones. They cut down trees and used the wood to build ships. They sold some of these goods to other colonies in America. Some of the goods were shipped back to England.

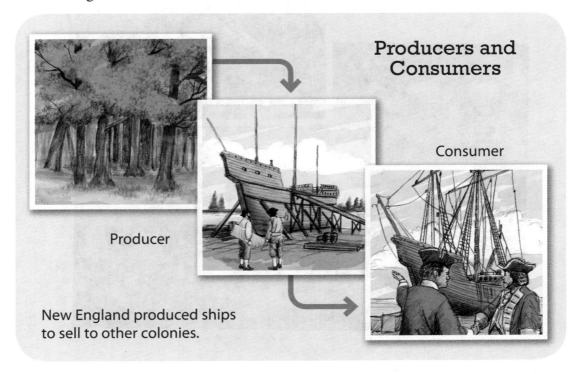

Producers and Consumers

Producer

Consumer

New England produced ships to sell to other colonies.

Families worked very hard in New England. Fathers ran their farms or worked at their **trades**. A trade is a job that takes special skill, like building ships or making tables and chairs. Fathers also prayed and read the Bible with their families.

Mothers worked at home. They cared for the children. They took care of the farm animals and the garden. They baked bread and cooked meals. Sometimes they made special things like cod chowder or cranberry pudding. In most homes, they made the clothes that their families wore.

Children learned to do many of the same jobs their parents did. In most families, there was not a lot of time to play.

In a Puritan church service, the people sang the Psalms.

On Sundays the whole family went to church. Church was held in a building called the **meetinghouse**. The pastor preached from the Bible. The people liked to hear God's Word. Sometimes they stayed after church and talked more about God and about the sermon.

The meetinghouse was also a place where citizens could have town meetings. A town meeting was a time to make decisions for the community. The men voted at the meetinghouse. Sometimes they talked about how to keep their town safe or how to care for the poor.

What natural resources did the New England colonists use?

Schools in New England

Many of the New England colonists had been given a good **education** in England. Education is training at home or in schools. The Puritans wanted their children to have a good education in the New World. They had a special reason for wanting this. They wanted their children to be able to read God's Word.

Most parents taught their own children. But sometimes a woman in the town taught children in her home. This was called a **dame school**. Children used a **hornbook** to learn to read and write. A hornbook had the letters of the alphabet on it. It also quoted the Lord's Prayer. Children sometimes wore the book on a string around their necks.

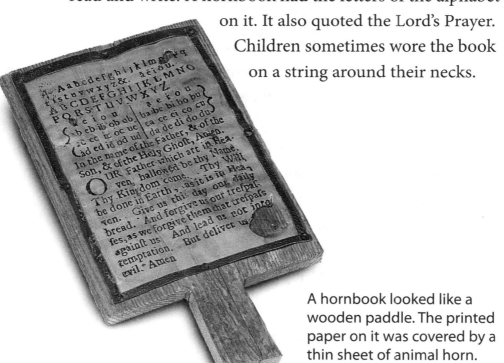

A hornbook looked like a wooden paddle. The printed paper on it was covered by a thin sheet of animal horn.

A Prospect of the Colledges in Cambridge in New England.

The larger towns had **grammar schools**. Each town paid the teacher of its school. Only boys went to grammar school. They studied Greek, Latin, and math. They learned to read, speak, and write well. They also learned more about the Bible.

The Puritan leaders wanted a place of education for young men after grammar school. They wanted it to be a place that taught how to preach God's Word. New England started the first **college** in the colonies. Harvard College was started for young men who wanted to be pastors. Harvard was in Massachusetts. This college is still open today.

Two New England Poets
Anne Bradstreet

Anne Bradstreet was a Puritan. She came to the New World with the group led by John Winthrop. She and her husband Simon settled in the town of Boston, Massachusetts.

Anne Bradstreet had been given a good education in England. She liked to write poems. She wrote about her life in the New World. Sometimes she wrote poems about her family. She and her husband had eight children. Almost all of her poems were about God.

Anne Bradstreet was the first woman in the New World to publish a book of poems.

Why did Puritans have a special interest in education?

Phillis Wheatley

A few families in New England owned slaves. Phillis was a slave in the home of the Wheatley family in Boston.

Unlike many slaves, Phillis Wheatley got an education. She learned to read and write. God had given her skill in writing poems. When she was only nineteen, she published some of her poems.

Phillis Wheatley lived more than one hundred years after Anne Bradstreet. She was the first African American woman to publish a book of poems.

Anne Bradstreet

- *from England*
- *lived in 1600s*
- *came to the New World as a free woman*

- *lived in Boston*
- *educated*
- *liked to write poems*
- *wrote about God*
- *published books*

Phillis Wheatley

- *from Africa*
- *lived in 1700s*
- *came to the New World as a slave*

The Great Awakening

As time passed, the churches in the colonies changed. Not everyone in the churches was a Christian. Even in New England many Puritans had lost their strong belief in God's Word.

People were living sinful lives. People needed to come back to God. Some pastors saw this great need. Jonathan Edwards was one of these pastors.

Edwards had a church in Massachusetts. He preached from the Bible. He told the people how God felt about their sin. God used Jonathan Edwards to show many people their sin. People got on their knees and prayed. They asked God to forgive them. Many people came back to God.

What pastor did God use to lead the Great Awakening?

This return to God in the colonies was called the **Great Awakening**. After the Great Awakening, more people wanted to tell others about God. David Brainerd wanted to tell the Indians of God's love. For four years he traveled and preached to the Indians. He died while he was still a young man. But because of him, many Indians heard God's Word and trusted Christ.

David Brainerd

"There is nothing in the world worth living for but . . . doing the work that Christ did."

Plymouth Massachusetts Bay
1620 1630

1600   1625 1636 1650   1675   1700   1725 1740s 1750
Harvard College   Great Awakening

O give thanks unto the Lord; for he is good. . . . [He] giveth food to all flesh: for his mercy endureth for ever.

— Psalm 136:1, 25

Focus

People from many different countries came to the middle colonies for religious freedom.

- apprentice
- Quaker
- religious freedom
- tradition

Activity

Gingerbread Man

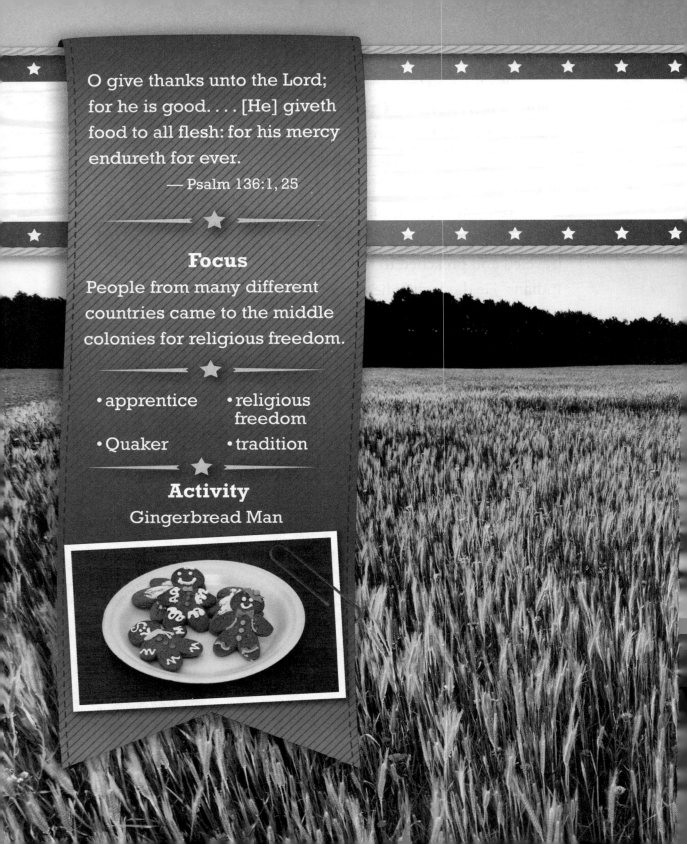

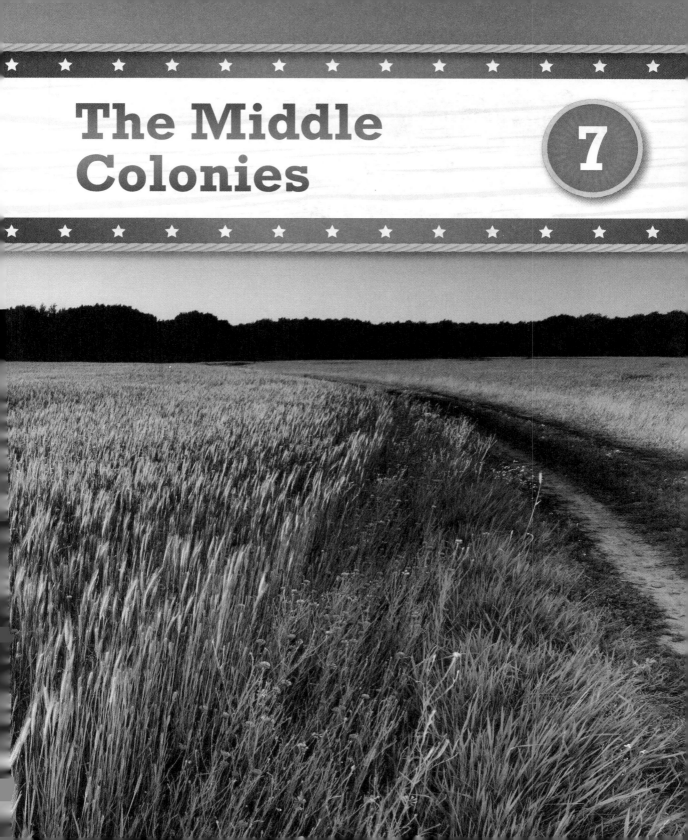

The Middle Colonies

7

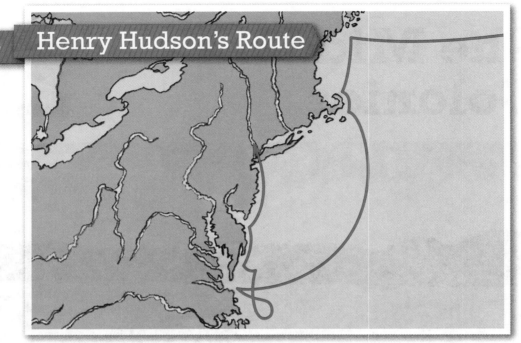

Henry Hudson's Route

The harbor and rivers in this region made it an ideal place for shipping and trade.

New York and New Jersey

The year was 1609. The colonists at Jamestown were settling into life in the New World. The Pilgrims and the Puritans were still living in Europe. And a man named Henry Hudson was exploring. He was working for a country in Europe called the Netherlands.

Hudson sailed along the American coast. He found a river that took him farther into the continent. Hudson claimed the region around the river for the Netherlands. The river came to be called the Hudson River after him.

About fifteen years later a group of Dutch colonists came to this region. The Dutch are people from the Netherlands. Their colony was called New Netherland. The Dutch government wanted these colonists to make money for their home country. They could earn money by trading and selling furs.

Some of the colonists settled along the river. Others settled on an island called Manhattan. Peter Minuit became their governor. These colonists bought the island from the Indians. Their settlement became very large.

Peter Minuit, the colony's governor, probably traded goods for the land.

The Netherlands was not the only country that claimed this region. England claimed it too. The English king's brother, the Duke of York, sent warships to Manhattan Island. But the Dutch did not want to fight a war. They turned their colony over to the English duke in peace. New Netherland then became known as New York.

The Duke of York gave part of his new land to his friends. They gave their land a different name. The southern part of New York became another colony called New Jersey.

Which two colonies were begun by the Dutch?

Pennsylvania

The **Quakers** were another group in England who did not agree with the Church of England. But the Quakers had a different religion than the Puritans did. They believed people have an "inner light" that shows them how to live. They trusted in this "inner light" more than they did the Bible. Quakers were not treated well in England.

William Penn was a Quaker. He saw how other people treated Quakers. He saw that many Quakers wanted to get away from England. Penn found a better place for people of his religion to live.

Psalm 119:105

Thy word is a lamp unto my feet, and a light unto my path.

The king of England owed money to William Penn's family. When Penn's father died, the king paid Penn back. He paid by giving him land in America. The land was covered with forest. The king called it Penn's Sylvania, which means "Penn's Woods."

William Penn sailed for America with other Quakers who wanted to leave. When they got to Pennsylvania, Penn made a wise choice. He knew that the king had said the land was his. But Penn paid the Indians for his land. They had been using that land for hundreds of years. Penn's choice to pay them helped him make friends with them.

The Quakers in Pennsylvania got to work right away. They cut down trees. They built homes. They set up their government. William Penn let the people choose their own leaders. He also wanted everyone in the colony to be treated justly. In England Quakers had been put in prison for their beliefs. In Pennsylvania no one could be sent to prison unless he had been blamed for a crime.

At first Pennsylvania was a colony only for Quakers. But Penn also wanted people of other religions to be free. He let Swedish, Dutch, and German people live in Pennsylvania. They were not Quakers. But they were free to worship as they chose. Penn made Pennsylvania a place of **religious freedom**.

The first Europeans in Pennsylvania were people of what religion?

William Penn

William Penn grew up in a wealthy English family. He had a college education. He was handsome, he wore fine clothes, and he loved to go to parties. But he changed his ways when he became a Quaker. Quakers believed people should dress plainly and live a simple life. Penn preached and wrote about his new religion. A few times he was even put in jail for preaching.

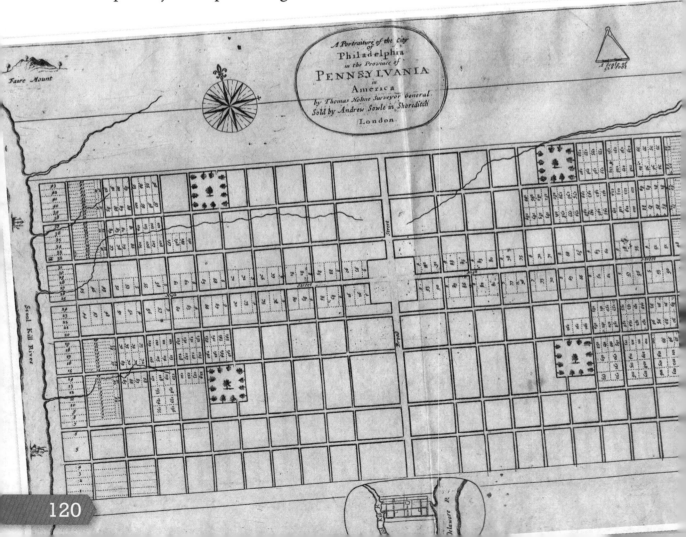

When Penn was granted the land of Pennsylvania, he began making plans. He wanted the colony to be a safe place for everyone. He wanted everyone to be free to choose how to worship. He drew up plans for a city called Philadelphia, the "City of Brotherly Love." Important buildings would be at the center of town. Homes would have their own gardens and fields. Wide streets left room for the city to grow.

Penn had married a Quaker woman named Guli. He had to leave her and their children behind when he sailed for Pennsylvania. He arrived in 1682. A small group of colonists who had come ahead of Penn were already building Philadelphia.

Penn built a house of his own. But he never spent much time living in it. He soon had to return to England. He had to settle problems about his land, and his wife was ill. The problems dragged on for many years. During that time, Penn's wife Guli died.

William Penn returned to Pennsylvania in 1699 with his second wife, Hannah. They were able to stay for only two years. But Penn saw that the colony had grown. Philadelphia was a large, busy city of several thousand people. Penn's plan for the city had been a success.

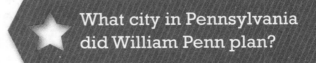

What city in Pennsylvania did William Penn plan?

Delaware

The southern part of William Penn's land was the area that is now Delaware. Before the land was Penn's, Swedes had settled there. Swedes are people from Sweden.

At first their colony was called New Sweden. The Dutch took over the colony, and then the English ruled it. The river in that area was called the Delaware River. It was named for an Englishman, Lord De La Warr. He was one of the governors of Jamestown. The colony was also called Delaware. Delaware did not become a separate colony until 1776.

The Middle Colonies

This map shows the four colonies along the middle part of America's east coast. New York, New Jersey, Pennsylvania, and Delaware were called the middle colonies.

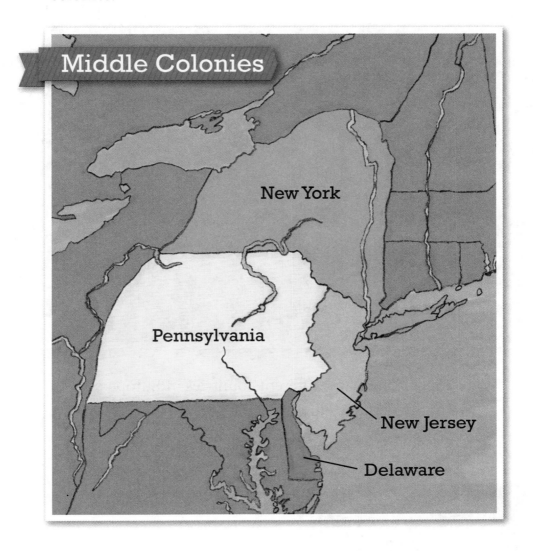

Middle Colonies

New York

Pennsylvania

New Jersey

Delaware

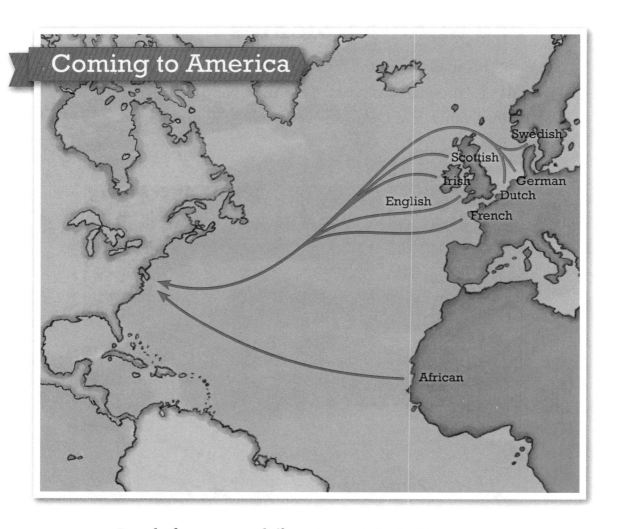

Coming to America

People from many different countries in Europe came to live in the middle colonies. Some people from Africa were also brought to the middle colonies as slaves.

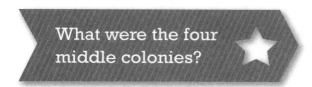

What were the four middle colonies?

Jobs in the Middle Colonies

The people of the middle colonies used their natural resources wisely. Many rivers flowed through the land. They made the soil rich. The flat plains also made the land easy to farm. Farming became one of the most important jobs in the middle colonies.

Farms were larger than those in New England. Colonists grew corn, oats, barley, and wheat. They sold these grains to the colonies north and south of them. They also built mills to grind grain into flour. Because the middle colonies produced so much grain, they were called the "Breadbasket Colonies."

The tricorn hat, worn in Europe and the colonies, was made from beaver felt.

Another job in the middle colonies was trapping animals. Beavers and otter lived along the rivers. Mink, lynx, and weasels lived in the woods. All of these animals were prized for their fur. Animal furs were used to make clothing and hats. Colonists trapped for furs themselves. They also traded with the Indians for more furs.

Grains, flour, furs, and wood from the forests were shipped to Europe. The income from these goods helped many of the colonists live in comfort.

People in Europe and America used grain to make flour for bread.

Many men in the middle colonies also worked at trades. Some built wagons, wheels, and barrels out of wood. Others made tools, kettles, nails, and horseshoes out of iron. Some made tableware out of silver. Some printed books and newspapers.

Not as many boys in the middle colonies went to college as those in New England. Often they wanted to learn a trade instead. These boys could become **apprentices**. An apprentice went to live with someone who knew a trade. He watched and learned and worked hard. After several years he knew the trade himself. When he was twenty-one, he could start his own shop or business.

Apprentice

John wants to learn to be a blacksmith. A blacksmith makes objects out of iron.

John becomes an apprentice to his father's friend, Mr. Rogers.

John helps Mr. Rogers make iron pots and tools.

John spends seven years learning at Mr. Rogers's blacksmith shop.

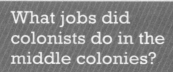
What jobs did colonists do in the middle colonies?

At age twenty-one John receives a set of blacksmithing tools from Mr. Rogers. John opens his own shop.

People from All Over

People in the middle colonies came from different countries. Each country had its own culture. The middle colonies were a "melting pot," or a blend, of many cultures.

The colonists built homes as soon as they could. They remembered the homes they had left behind in their old countries. The new homes looked very much like their old homes. Different kinds of homes filled the middle colonies.

French

English

Dutch

Swedish

German

The people who came to the middle colonies brought many new **traditions** with them. A tradition is a special way of doing something for many years.

The Puritans in the New England colonies did not celebrate Christmas. But many people in the middle colonies did. The Dutch baked small Christmas cakes and gave us our word for *cookies*. Over time, the gingerbread cookie became a Christmas tradition in the colonies. Germans brought with them the tradition of giving gifts. Much later in the 1800s, they were the first to have Christmas trees in their homes.

Henry Hudson
1609

Pennsylvania
1682

1600   1650 1664   1700   1750   1776   1800
        New York   Delaware

The middle colonies were a safe place for people of different religions. For this reason there were different kinds of churches in the middle colonies. Dutch, German, and English people had their own churches. There was even a place of worship for Jews in New York.

Most people in the middle colonies went to a church. Many true Christians lived there. But many more did not know Christ.

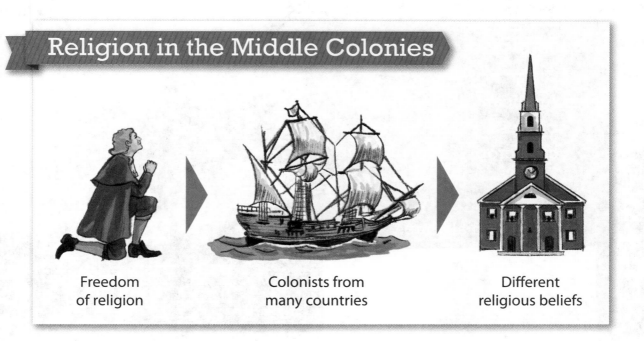

Religion in the Middle Colonies

Freedom of religion

Colonists from many countries

Different religious beliefs

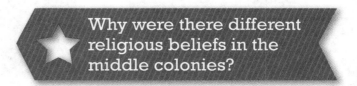

Why were there different religious beliefs in the middle colonies?

> He maketh his sun to rise on the evil and on the good, and sendeth rain on the just and on the unjust.
>
> — Matthew 5:45

Focus

People in the southern colonies depended on cash crops to make a living.

- Anglican
- burgess
- cash crop
- Catholic
- debtor
- plantation

Activity

Colonial Shops

The Southern Colonies

8

Virginia

Jamestown was the first English colony in the New World to last. More and more people came to live there. Jamestown began to spread out. The settlement that had been Jamestown was now part of a larger colony. The colony came to be called Virginia.

Many of the people who settled in Virginia became farmers. Tobacco was the main crop they grew. The colonists had learned about the plant from the Indians. Some people in England and the colonies wanted tobacco. Others believed smoking tobacco was bad for a person's health. Even King James spoke against it.

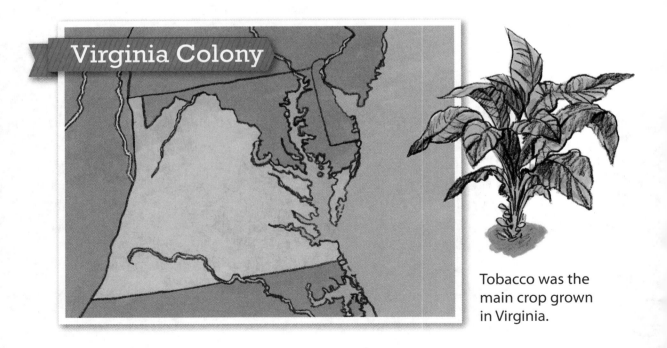

Virginia Colony

Tobacco was the main crop grown in Virginia.

Virginia was the first colony to choose its own leaders. The English king was over the colony. But the colonists had the right to make their own local laws. Colonists elected people called **burgesses** to make their laws. This group of leaders was called the House of Burgesses. Many other colonies later had groups like this one.

Jamestown was the capital of Virginia. But near the end of the 1600s, a fire burned much of the city. The capital was then moved to the city of Williamsburg.

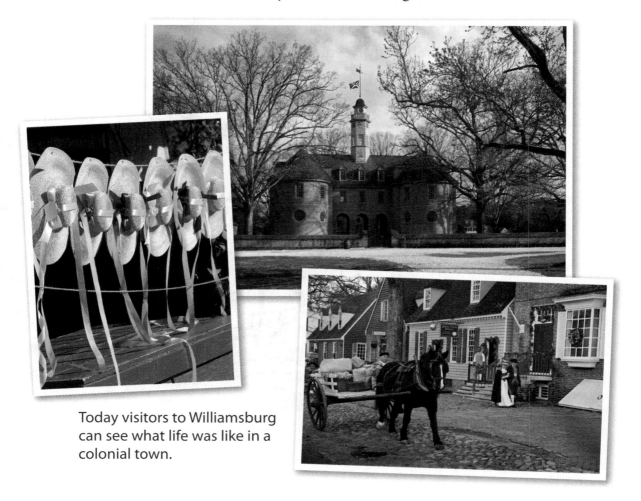

Today visitors to Williamsburg can see what life was like in a colonial town.

Maryland

Quakers, Puritans, and Pilgrims had all left England because of their religious beliefs. Now another group wanted to leave. **Catholics** also did not agree with the Church of England. One Catholic man, George Calvert, was a friend of the king. The king gave him a gift of land in the New World. The land was called Maryland. Calvert wanted it to be a safe place for Catholics to live and worship.

The first settlers built a city in Maryland called Saint Mary's. Soon Maryland became a place of religious freedom, even for people who were not Catholics.

What was the first colony to choose its own leaders?

Today we know Charles Towne as the city of Charleston, South Carolina.

The Carolinas

Charles II had been at war with the other leaders of England. When he finally became king, he gave a gift to those who had been on his side in the war. He gave eight men a large piece of land in America. The men named the colony Carolina.

One group of English colonists settled in the southern part of Carolina. These colonists formed a town that they named after the king. It was called Charles Towne. Charles Towne was on the coast. It was a fine **port**, a place where ships come and go. Charles Towne became a center of trade in the southern colonies.

The southern Carolina colonists began to grow rice. The warm, wet climate in the south was very good for rice plants. Some farms in the south grew very large. These large farms were called **plantations**.

Another group of colonists settled in northern Carolina. They lived much closer to the colony of Virginia. Like the men in Virginia, many of these colonists grew tobacco.

After fifty years, the colony of Carolina split into two colonies. The northern part was called North Carolina, and the southern part was South Carolina.

Rice was grown in the warmer parts of the southern colonies.

What were the large farms in the southern colonies called?

Eliza Pinckney

Eliza Pinckney lived in South Carolina in the 1700s. Her father was an officer in England's army. He owned three plantations. During a war, he had to go to the islands of the West Indies. His wife's poor health made her unable to care for the family. He left Eliza, age sixteen, in charge of his plantations.

Eliza did her job well. She loved to study plants. Her father sent her some new seeds from the islands. They were from a plant called **indigo**, which was used to make blue dye. Eliza learned how to grow and care for indigo. She began to share indigo seeds with her neighbors. Before long, many other plantations were growing indigo. It became the most successful crop in the South after rice.

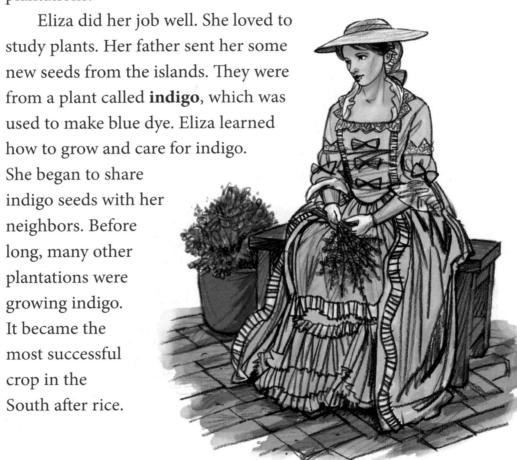

Georgia

A man in England named James Oglethorpe wanted to help prisoners. People who were **debtors** had to go to prison. A debtor is a person who owes money to someone else. While a debtor was in prison, he could not work to earn money. England's prisons made it hard for the poor to repay their debts. Oglethorpe wanted to start a colony where debtors could live and work. Then they could pay back their debts.

King George liked Oglethorpe's plan. He gave him the land south of the Carolinas. The colony would be called Georgia after the king.

The first settlers went to Georgia in 1733. Some were debtors, but most were not. Georgia was the last English colony formed in the New World.

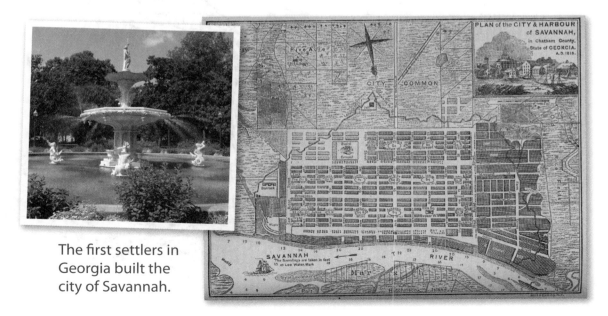

The first settlers in Georgia built the city of Savannah.

James Oglethorpe

James Oglethorpe grew up near London, England. He was educated at Oxford and became a leader in the English government. One of Oglethorpe's friends was put in prison because of his debts. The man came down with a disease in prison. He grew worse and worse, and finally he died. Oglethorpe began working to give debtors like his friend a better life.

Oglethorpe took 114 people with him to the Georgia colony. He wanted the colony to honor God. He made laws against slavery and drinking liquor. Oglethorpe made friends with the Indians and treated them with respect. He built forts and helped defend the colony against the Spanish in nearby Florida.

Georgia was owned by the king. Oglethorpe could not hold a government position there. But most Georgia settlers thought of him as their first governor.

The Southern Colonies

This map shows the five colonies along the southeast coast of America. Virginia, Maryland, North and South Carolina, and Georgia were called the southern colonies.

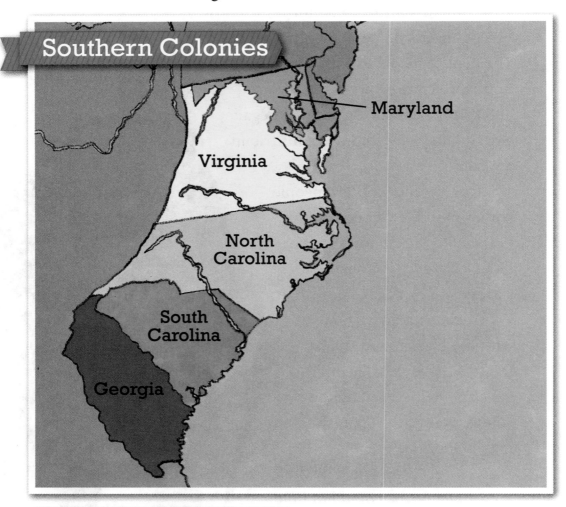

Southern Colonies

Maryland

Virginia

North Carolina

South Carolina

Georgia

What were the five southern colonies?

Farming in the Southern Colonies

Farming was the most important job in the southern colonies. This region had rich soil and a warm climate. Crops grew well there. They could be grown more months out of the year than in other colonies.

People in Europe wanted tobacco, rice, and indigo. Farmers in the southern colonies saw that they could earn a good income through selling crops. They began to grow these three crops in large numbers. They shipped most of them across the ocean to Europe.

Crops were often taken by river to one of the southern ports to be shipped to Europe.

People in the southern colonies depended on their crops to make money. They called these important crops **cash crops**.

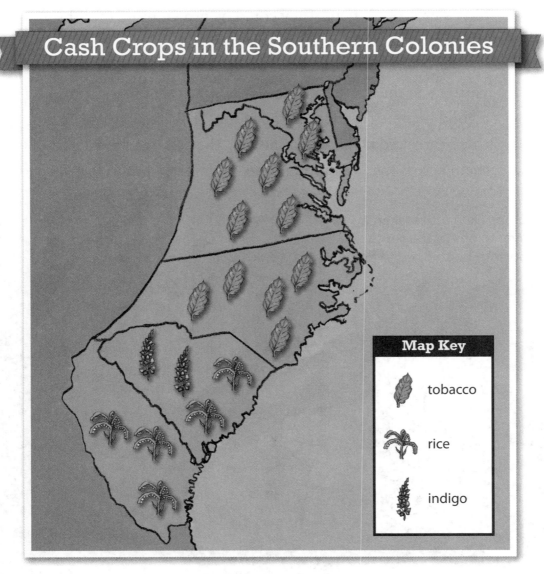

Cash Crops in the Southern Colonies

Map Key

tobacco

rice

indigo

This map shows the three main cash crops and where they were grown.

Some farms grew into plantations because of the need to plant so many crops. The owners needed large numbers of workers to care for their fields. Plantation owners used thousands of Africans to work as slaves in their colonies. They wanted slaves because they could be bought and owned. Once a colonist had bought a slave, he could keep him for the rest of his life.

Some colonists who owned plantations became very wealthy. The largest plantations were like small communities.

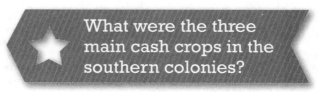

What were the three main cash crops in the southern colonies?

Plantations were like small communities. They were usually built near a river.

1. The **main house** was where the owner and his family lived.

2. Cooking was usually done by slaves in another building to protect the house from fire.

3. Meat was salted and smoked in a **smokehouse** to make it last longer, since there was no way to keep it cold or frozen.

4. Barns and **storehouses** held crops waiting to be shipped and sold.

5. The family's horses were kept in the **stables**. Some plantations even had their own blacksmiths. A large plantation might keep several carriages in its **carriage house**.

6. Slaves lived in small **cabins** with dirt floors. Large plantations like this one might have housed hundreds of slaves.

7. Slaves washed clothes and linens for the owner's family in the **laundry house**. Clothes were soaked in a huge tub of boiling water and then rubbed on a washboard. They were wrung out by hand before being hung to dry.

Slaves on Plantations

Life was hard for the slaves on plantations. Most slaves came from West Africa. There they had lived in close family groups. But when they were taken to America, many did not get to stay with their families. A man might be sold to one plantation, and his wife to another.

Planting and caring for the crops was hard work. Slaves had to work long hours in all kinds of weather. Most slaves worked in the fields, but some of them did housework for the owner. Even children did small jobs like carrying water and pulling weeds. Slaves received little, if any, pay for their work. They were given their food, clothing, and a place to live.

Most slaves tried to make the best of their hard lives. They treated other slaves like family. They learned to make special dishes from the food they were given. They told stories and sang songs. Many Africans became Christians in America. Their songs were about Jesus and the freedom He gives to people. We still remember and sing some of these songs today.

Many colonists did not believe it was right to own slaves. Most Quakers and some Puritans did not keep slaves. They wrote and spoke against slavery. The smaller farms in the southern colonies did not use slaves to do their work. But most plantation owners felt that they could not do without their slaves.

Some slaves wove beautiful baskets like the one on the chair in this cabin.

What kind of work did slaves do on plantations?

Religion in the Southern Colonies

All the southern colonies were first settled by people from England. Most of these colonists belonged to the Church of England. They were called **Anglicans**. They went to the Anglican church nearest them. Maryland was the only colony where Catholics were the first settlers.

African slaves were not always able to go to church. Some of them went to church where their owners did. But they were not treated the same as their owners. In some churches they had to sit at the back or even outside.

Small groups of French colonists also came to the southern colonies. Many of these were Christians who could not worship freely in France. They were called **Huguenots**. One group of Huguenots settled in Virginia. Another group settled in South Carolina.

Many Huguenots had been craftsmen in France. They brought special skills with them to the colonies. Some were silk weavers. Others made glass, clocks, and watches. More importantly, they brought with them a strong faith in Christ.

The oldest Huguenot church in America today is in Charleston, South Carolina.

What religious group did most southern colonists belong to?

Education in the Southern Colonies

Children in the southern colonies were usually taught at home. Parents often taught their own children. Some wealthy parents hired a teacher who lived in their home.

Colonists in Virginia built the first college in the southern colonies. It was called the College of William and Mary. Unlike the New England colleges, it was not a school only for pastors. It was the first college in America to have a law school.

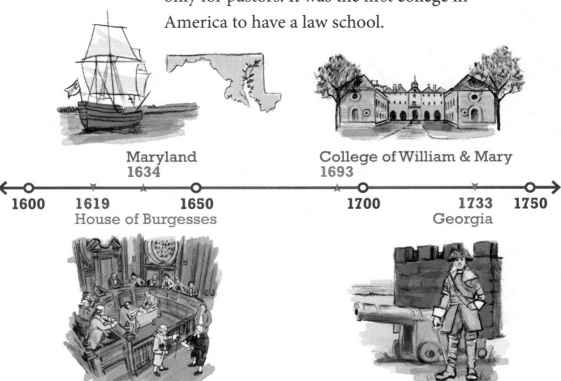

Maryland
1634

College of William & Mary
1693

1600   1619   1650   1700   1733   1750
     House of Burgesses   Georgia

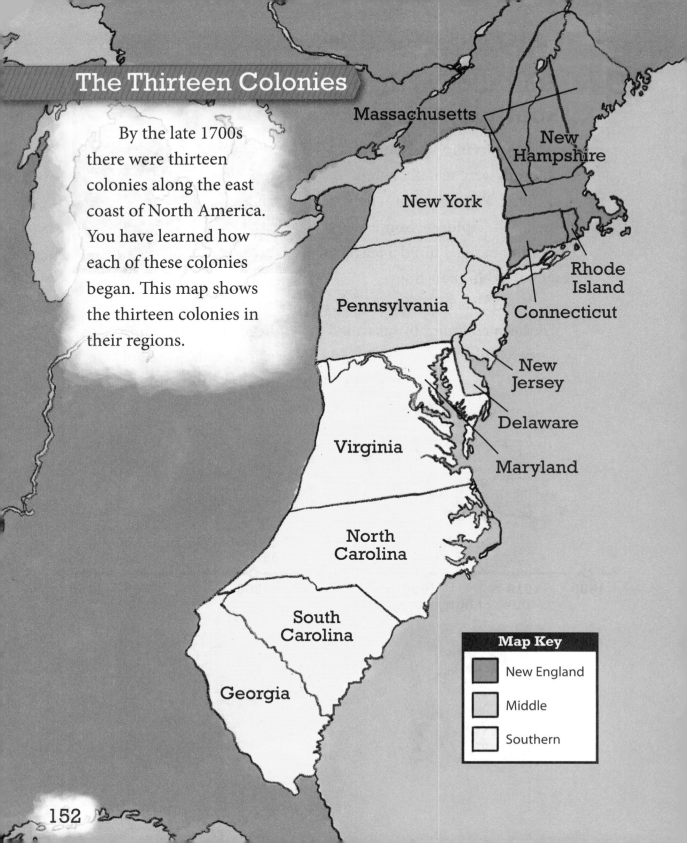

The Thirteen Colonies

By the late 1700s there were thirteen colonies along the east coast of North America. You have learned how each of these colonies began. This map shows the thirteen colonies in their regions.

Massachusetts

New Hampshire

New York

Rhode Island

Connecticut

Pennsylvania

New Jersey

Delaware

Maryland

Virginia

North Carolina

South Carolina

Georgia

Map Key	
	New England
	Middle
	Southern

Three Colonial Regions

	New England Colonies	Middle Colonies	Southern Colonies
Colonists	mostly English	English, Dutch, Swedish, German, French, Scottish, and Africans	mostly English and Africans, some French
Religion	mostly Puritans	many different religions	mostly Anglicans
Education	dame schools and grammar schools, first college	church schools	home education, first law school
Jobs	shipbuilding, fishing, making furniture	grain farming, fur trapping, trades	cash crop farming, trades

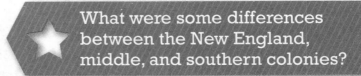

What were some differences between the New England, middle, and southern colonies?

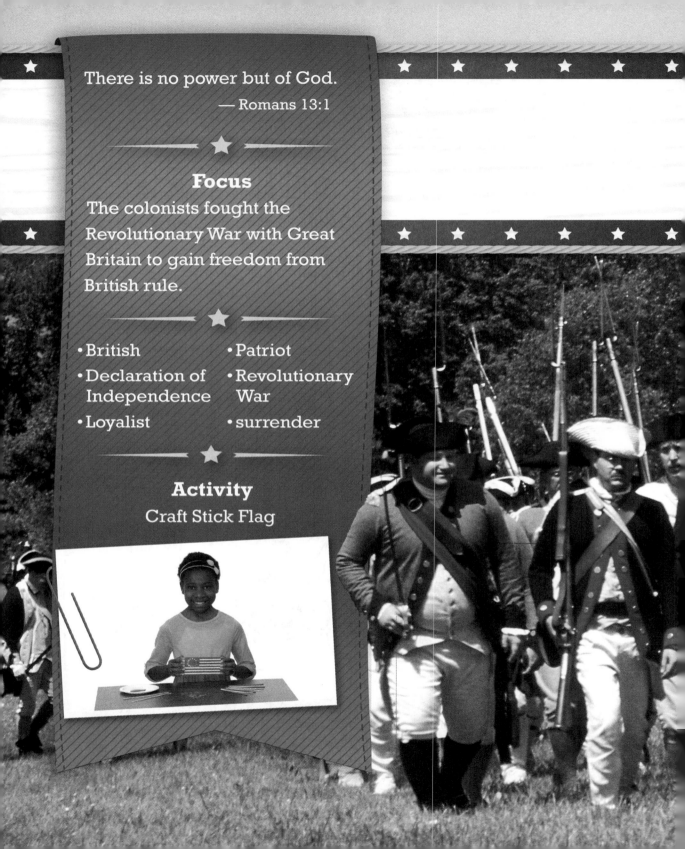

> There is no power but of God.
> — Romans 13:1

Focus

The colonists fought the Revolutionary War with Great Britain to gain freedom from British rule.

- British
- Declaration of Independence
- Loyalist
- Patriot
- Revolutionary War
- surrender

Activity

Craft Stick Flag

The Revolutionary War

9

The French and Indian War

Colonists now lived all along the Atlantic coast in North America. Many of these colonists were from England. Some were also from Scotland, Ireland, and Wales. These four countries together were called Great Britain. They were all under the same ruler. Citizens of these countries were known as the **British**.

The British were not the only settlers in the New World. You have read that colonists also came from other countries in Europe. Many settlers had come from the country of France. Some French people lived in the thirteen colonies. Many more lived west and north of the colonies. They lived in places that were good for fur trading.

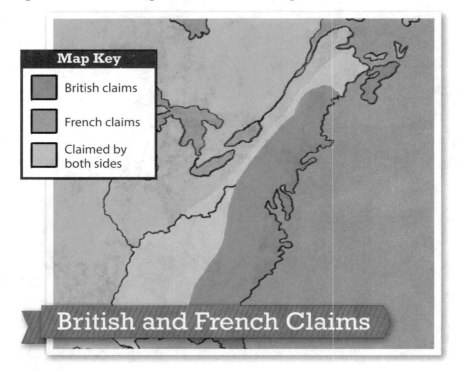

Map Key

- British claims
- French claims
- Claimed by both sides

British and French Claims

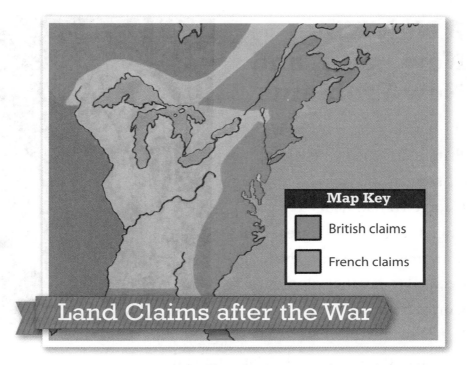

Land Claims after the War

France and Great Britain both wanted to rule over North America. They both wanted to own all the land. They both wanted the goods produced there. They could not settle the problem, and war began.

Part of this war took place in America. It was called the **French and Indian War**. Most of the Indians fought on the French side. The Iroquois, however, fought on the British side. Many of the colonists fought for the British too.

The war lasted seven years. The British finally won. Great Britain gained more land in the New World than it ever had before.

Which two countries fought over land in the New World?

A New King, New Laws, and New Problems

During the war Great Britain crowned a new king. As soon as the war ended, King George III had debts to pay. England had spent a great deal of money on the war. The king decided to tax the colonies to gain extra money.

Now the colonists had to pay taxes on many goods from England. There were new taxes on paper, glass, lead, paint, and tea.

The British government also left soldiers in the colonies to keep order. Another new law said that the colonists must give these British soldiers food and a place to stay.

Many of the colonists were angry about the new laws. They were not used to paying taxes to the British government. They had not been allowed to vote on the new tax laws. Keeping the British soldiers in their towns cost them extra money. They felt that the British government was taking too much control over them.

But other colonists thought they should obey the laws and not get angry. "King George is still our king," they said. "God gave him the right to rule over us."

Some colonists were afraid. They had family in Great Britain. They did not want to do anything that would cause trouble for their families.

Why were many colonists angry about the new laws?

The Boston Massacre

The British army sent soldiers to the city of Boston, Massachusetts. The colonists in Boston had caused trouble for Great Britain. King George thought the soldiers would calm the city down.

But that is not what happened. Colonists mocked and shouted at the soldiers. Sometimes they threw eggs or rocks at them. The soldiers shouted back. They sometimes got into fights with the colonists.

The worst thing happened one night in 1770. Some men and boys threw snowballs and stones at the soldiers. The soldiers fired their guns into the crowd. Five people were killed. The colonists called the killing a **massacre**. *Massacre* means "the killing of many people."

One of the people killed was Crispus Attucks, an African American.

A Tea Party in Boston Harbor

Things quieted down for a while. The British government decided to do away with most of the taxes. But the tax on tea stayed the same. Three years after the Boston Massacre, England shipped two thousand chests of tea to the colonies. More than three hundred tea chests came to Boston.

The colonists loved to drink tea. But they did not want to pay the tax. If they paid it, they would be agreeing that the tax was fair and right. Many believed it was not fair.

In Boston, the citizens asked their governor to send the tea back to England. But he would not do it. Some of the colonists formed a plan.

Late one night men and boys from Boston met at the harbor. They wore blankets and carried axes. They had smeared paint and soot on their faces to make themselves look like Indians.

The men boarded the British ships that held the chests of tea. With their axes they broke open each chest. They dumped the tea into the ocean. They hoped the king would now understand how the colonists felt about the tax.

Why did the colonists throw the tea into Boston Harbor?

Patriot: The king does not understand or listen to us. He wants to take away the freedom God gave us. We should be able to make our own laws. We should not have to pay taxes we did not vote for.

News of the "tea party" quickly spread throughout the thirteen colonies. Colonists began taking sides. Some of them wanted to stay true, or loyal, to the king and to Great Britain. They were called **Loyalists**. Others wanted to throw off British rule. They were even ready to fight for their freedom if they had to. They were called **Patriots**.

The British were not happy about the Boston Tea Party. They made a new law that closed the port of Boston. No ships could come in or go out. The British also took away some of the colonists' rights. Citizens of Massachusetts could no longer choose their leaders. They could not hold any more town meetings.

Loyalist: The British army has kept us safe in the New World. Paying taxes is only fair. The British king is the ruler God gave us. We should honor and obey him.

Headed for War

Leaders from nearly every colony met in the city of Philadelphia. They talked about what to do. They made a list of their complaints against Great Britain. They sent it to the king.

Most of the men did not want the colonies to go to war against Great Britain. But some were afraid there was no other way to settle the problems.

King George did not want a war either. But he did not want to give in. He believed the colonists were wrong. They were British citizens, and he was their king. He felt that they must be made to obey.

The colonists began to gather guns. They stored them in the town of Concord. They wanted to be ready to fight. The British general, Thomas Gage, heard about the guns. He sent seven hundred soldiers to find and destroy them.

A silversmith from Boston named Paul Revere found out about the soldiers' plans. He jumped on his horse and rode toward Concord. Along the way, he warned other colonists, "The British are coming!" Young men called **minutemen** took up their guns. Minutemen were ready to fight at any minute.

Near Concord was the town of Lexington. The British soldiers marched there first. But the colonists were ready for them.

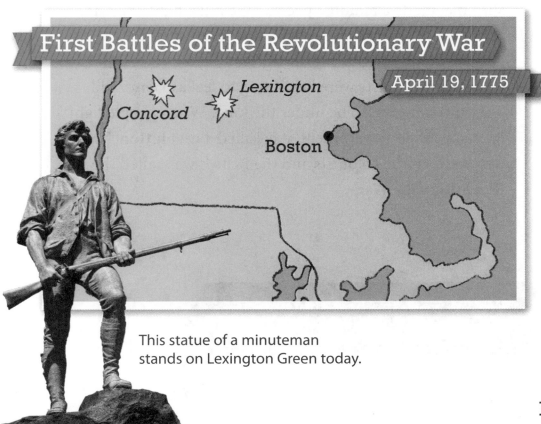

First Battles of the Revolutionary War

April 19, 1775

Concord

Lexington

Boston

This statue of a minuteman stands on Lexington Green today.

Patrick Henry

About seventy minutemen waited on Lexington Green. British soldiers lined up facing them. No one knows who fired the first shot. But both sides fired. Some men were killed. War between the colonies and Great Britain had begun.

Some colonial leaders had begun to speak out about war. Patrick Henry, a lawyer and a Patriot from Virginia, made a famous speech. "We must fight," he said. "I know not what course others may take, but as for me, give me liberty or give me death!"

Other colonists were beginning to feel as Henry did. They did not want to be under the king. When people fight to change their government, it is called a **revolution**. The war between the colonists and the British was called the **Revolutionary War**.

Where were the first shots of the Revolutionary War fired?

The Declaration of Independence

The leaders from each colony met for a second time. They decided that they needed their own army. They chose George Washington to be its commander.

George Washington was a planter from Virginia. He was a member of the House of Burgesses. He was also a soldier. He had fought bravely in the French and Indian War. Four bullets had torn through his coat, and two horses had been shot out from under him.

Washington went to Boston to lead the army. His job would not be easy. The British army was large and strong. The colonists' army was not well trained. But they were brave and wanted to fight.

George Washington was a brave soldier and a good leader.

The colonists also needed to put their plans into writing. It was time to **declare**, or make known, that they were free from Great Britain. The same men who had chosen Washington to lead the army now had to choose someone to write down their plans.

They chose Thomas Jefferson, a skilled writer. Jefferson worked on the paper for several weeks. He wrote about rights and freedom. He said God had created all people with certain rights. A good government should protect those rights. It should not take them away. The paper he wrote was called the **Declaration of Independence**.

Americans still celebrate Independence Day every year on July 4.

The leaders talked about the paper and made some small changes to it. All thirteen colonies voted to accept the Declaration. On **July 4, 1776**, the Declaration of Independence was **adopted**, or accepted. The men signed their names on the paper.

The Declaration of Independence was printed. Copies were sent to the other colonies. A copy was taken to George Washington and the army. The soldiers cheered when they heard it read.

Now many colonists no longer thought of themselves as British citizens living in America. They thought of themselves as Americans.

What paper made the colonies' freedom known?

Battles Lost and Won

Early in the war Washington's army drove the British out of Boston. American soldiers had taken over two British forts in northern New York. They dragged huge cannons from the forts into Massachusetts. They took them to the hills. They pointed the cannons down at the city of Boston. The British soldiers did not want to fight against guns that big. They fled in their ships.

The next battles were in New York. The British had thousands of soldiers, many more than the Americans had. Washington and his men fought bravely. But they could not win. They had to leave New York.

Washington's army went to New Jersey. On Christmas Day in 1776, they crossed the icy Delaware River. They won a battle at the town of Trenton the next day.

The British had a new plan. The three parts of their army would meet in New York. They would cut off New England from the rest of the colonies. If they could win the war in the northern colonies, they would have an easier time winning in the south.

But the plan did not work. Not all of the British forces made it to the meeting place. One part of their army took over the city of Philadelphia and stopped there. At the Battle of Saratoga in New York, the British lost to the Americans.

The Battle of Saratoga gave the Americans hope. It made them feel that they could win the war. After this battle, France joined the American side in the war.

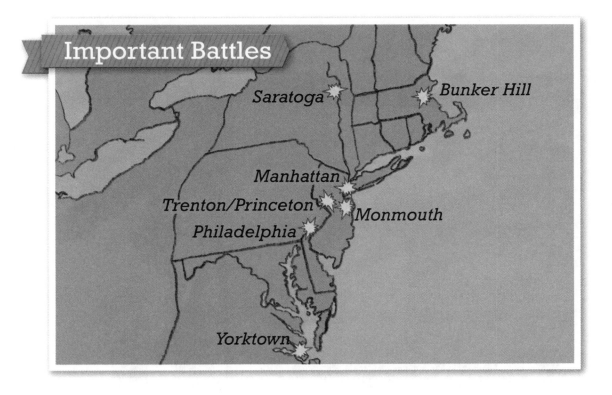

Important Battles

Saratoga

Bunker Hill

Manhattan

Trenton/Princeton

Monmouth

Philadelphia

Yorktown

Winter had come. The fighting stopped for a while. Washington's men were cold and tired. Their clothes and shoes were worn out. Many of them were sick. During the long winter at Valley Forge, Pennsylvania, about two thousand American soldiers died.

A German officer named Baron von Steuben joined the American army. He had fought in other wars and knew how to train soldiers. "Stand tall and move in a straight line," he told them. "Make sure you look clean and neat." He drilled Washington's men in marching and shooting. The soldiers began to feel braver and happier every day.

Von Steuben taught the American soldiers to use a weapon called a bayonet.

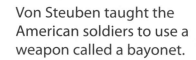
What battle made the Americans hopeful about winning the war?

The War Ends

After their winter at Valley Forge, the Americans were stronger and better trained. They heard that the British army was leaving Philadelphia. American troops hurried to the city and took it back.

The main part of Washington's army marched after the British soldiers. They caught up with them in New Jersey. There they fought the Battle of Monmouth.

A woman named Molly Pitcher became famous during the battle. Molly had been carrying water to the American soldiers. It was a hot day, and her husband felt too faint to load his cannon. Molly loaded it for him. She stood and fought bravely in his place.

People Who Fought on Each Side

British Army	British Loyalists	Germans	many Native Americans	some African Americans
American Army	Patriots	French	some Native Americans	some African Americans

Not all colonists fought in the war. Some did not want to take sides.

The Americans fought hard at Monmouth, but they did not stop the British. The British army marched on to New York. Then they headed farther south.

The rest of the war took place in the southern colonies. Many Loyalists lived in the South. The British thought they would have more colonists on their side there.

In 1781 the British and American forces met in Virginia. The French sent ships to help the Americans. The American army had many more soldiers than the British. The British army was trapped. At the Battle of Yorktown, the British **surrendered**, or gave up the fight, to the Americans. Washington's army watched as the British soldiers laid down their guns.

Yorktown was the last big battle of the Revolutionary War. Soon it was clear to everyone that the Americans had won.

Two years later, the British and the Americans signed the **Treaty of Paris**. The war was over. A new country called the United States of America was about to be born.

French and Indian War ends
1763

Revolutionary War begins
1775

British surrender at Yorktown
1781

1760   1770   1773   1776   1780   1790

Boston Tea Party

Declaration of Independence

John Adams

One of the men chosen to help form the Treaty of Paris was John Adams. Adams was born in Massachusetts in 1735. He went to Harvard College. He was a lawyer and a thinker. He wanted to help the colonies become free of British rule.

Adams married Abigail Smith. They had a very happy marriage. Abigail Adams helped her husband. He often asked her advice about decisions. Whenever they were apart, they wrote letters. These letters show us how much they loved and trusted each other. They also show us what life was like during the time of the Revolutionary War.

John Adams

Thomas Jefferson

Adams had been a strong leader on the Patriots' side all through the war. He had helped choose George Washington to lead the army. He had helped choose Thomas Jefferson to write the Declaration of Independence. He was one of the men who signed the Declaration. He was wise, and people trusted him. When the war was over, he again proved his skill as an American leader by his work on the peace treaty.

John Adams became the second president of the United States. Many years later his son, John Quincy Adams, became the sixth president.

Adams and Jefferson were good friends. They died on the same day—July 4, 1826. Exactly fifty years had passed since they had led their country in adopting the Declaration of Independence.

When the righteous are in authority, the people rejoice: but when the wicked beareth rule, the people mourn.

— Proverbs 29:2

Focus

The United States of America became a great nation by God's grace.

- Constitution
- House
- republic
- Senate

Activity

Wax Museum

A Nation Is Born 10

From Colonies to Country

The Revolutionary War was over. But the thirteen colonies had many plans and changes to make. They were not really colonies anymore. They were thirteen free states, or little countries, each with its own government. These thirteen separate states were also part of a new country. And the country needed a national government.

During the war, the leaders of each colony had met and made decisions. They called themselves the Continental Congress.

The second Continental Congress

The Continental Congress had realized that they needed a written plan of government. They chose a group of colonial leaders to write this new plan. John Dickinson, a leader from Delaware, did most of the writing. The new plan of government was called the **Articles of Confederation**. A confederation is a group of states joined together to help each other. The Articles named the confederation the United States of America.

The Articles were written before the war ended. But the states could not all agree on the Articles until after the war.

John Dickinson and the Articles of Confederation

 Why did Americans need a new plan of government?

Writing the Constitution

The Articles of Confederation worked for a while. But Americans needed a better plan. Under the Articles their government was too weak.

American leaders saw that their national government needed more power. It needed the power to tax. It needed the power to raise an army and fight wars. It needed to be able to settle problems about land with the Indians and with other countries.

But they also knew they did not want the government to have too much control. That was what they felt Great Britain had once had. That was why they had fought the Revolutionary War.

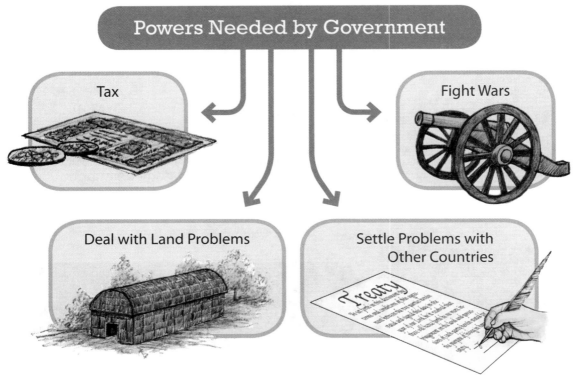

Powers Needed by Government

Tax

Fight Wars

Deal with Land Problems

Settle Problems with Other Countries

The Constitutional Convention

In 1787 the leaders met again in Philadelphia. Their job was to write a new plan of government. Men from every state except Rhode Island came. George Washington was in charge of the meetings. The leaders worked on the plan for several months.

The new plan was called the **Constitution**. The Constitution is one of the most important writings in America's history.

Why did the leaders meet in 1787?

Famous Leaders Who Formed the Constitution

Leader	State	Background
George Washington	Virginia	Commanded the American army in the Revolutionary War
James Madison	Virginia	Helped write Virginia's constitution
Benjamin Franklin	Pennsylvania	Worked for the American side in Great Britain and France during the Revolutionary War
Alexander Hamilton	New York	Served under Washington in the Revolutionary War

The Great Compromise

The Constitution's plan was for a new kind of government. This new government was called a **republic**. In a republic, citizens choose their leaders. But there are limits to the amount of power the leaders can have.

A problem came up while the Constitution was being written. The Constitution said that people in each state could choose leaders. Those leaders would then meet and vote about laws for the country. Each leader would get one vote. But how many votes should each state have?

The men did not want any one state to have too much control. Some states had more people living in them than others did. Should those states choose more leaders so that they would get more votes than the others? Or should each state get an equal number of votes?

Different men had different ideas. As the leader, George Washington listened to each man's plan. It seemed that they would never be able to agree. Then Washington called on a man named Roger Sherman. Sherman had thought of a wise way to make both sides happy.

Sherman said the government could have two groups of leaders who made laws. One group would have an equal number of leaders from each state. It would be called the **Senate**. The other group's number of leaders would be decided by the number of people in each state. That would mean states with more people would have more votes. This group of leaders would be called the **House**.

Roger Sherman

Today the Senate and the House meet in the Capitol.

Washington saw the wisdom of Sherman's plan. He called for a vote. More men voted yes than no. The plan passed. Sherman's plan was called the **Great Compromise.** A compromise is a way to solve an argument so that the people on both sides are happy.

Whose idea was the Great Compromise?

The Constitution Is Adopted

On September 17, 1787, the Constitution was finished. The many months of meetings had ended. It was time for the leaders to sign the Constitution and go back to their home states.

But even though the Constitution was finished, it was still not ready to be used. It had been written by a few men from each state. The rest of the people had not had a chance to vote on it. Now each state had to accept it. The people in each state had to agree that it was fair. They had to decide to live by its laws.

The men went back to their states with a big job to do. They had worked hard on the Constitution. They believed that it was good and fair. But each man had to help the people in his state see it that way too.

Some leaders who had worked on the Constitution wrote about its ideas. Their writings were printed in the newspapers. They were later made into a book. The writings helped many people understand the new kind of government.

Today we call these writings the *Federalist Papers*. They were written by Alexander Hamilton, James Madison, and John Jay.

Some people were not happy with the Constitution as it was. "The Constitution gives the government powers," they said. "But it does not list the people's rights." Even some of the leaders who had worked on the Constitution agreed. A **Bill of Rights**, a list of the people's freedoms, needed to be added to the Constitution.

Nine out of thirteen states had to accept the Constitution for it to be adopted. Some states agreed to accept it only if it had a Bill of Rights. New Hampshire was the ninth state to accept it. The Constitution was put in place early in 1789. Later the Bill of Rights was added to it. By 1790 all thirteen states had accepted it.

The Bill of Rights protects people's freedom to worship God and tell others about Him.

What had to be added to the Constitution so people would be happy with it?

A New Government

The new government would have a president, not a king. A president would be different from a king. He would lead the government. But he would be chosen by the people. He would be president for a set time, not for life. Presidents would serve for periods of four years called **terms.**

George Washington was chosen to be the first president of the United States. He started his first term in 1789. He chose good leaders to help him with his responsibilities.

George Washington

"I will faithfully [serve as] President of the United States, and will . . . preserve, protect, and defend the Constitution." (presidential oath)

Every United States president takes this oath. Presidents add the words "So help me God" at the end of the oath.

George Washington

George Washington was born in Virginia in 1732. His childhood was spent on farms. As a teen he spent much of his time on his half-brother Lawrence's farm, Mount Vernon. After Lawrence died, Mount Vernon became Washington's home.

George Washington was good at math and loved the outdoors. As a young man he worked as a surveyor, someone who measures land areas and draws maps and plans. He was also an officer in the Virginia militia.

Washington fought in the French and Indian War. Because he had courage and leadership skills, he was made a colonel. He was placed in command of all Virginia's forces.

After the war he married a widow named Martha Custis who had two children. The family settled at Mount Vernon.

A member of the House of Burgesses, Washington was very interested in the growing struggle with Great Britain. He felt that some British laws were unfair to planters like him. He agreed with the Patriots rather than the Loyalists.

Washington was elected to both the first and second Continental Congresses. As commander of the American army during the Revolutionary War, he was known for his calm, steady manner and wise decisions.

When it came time to choose America's first president, George Washington received every single vote. Although he was uneasy about the job before him, his fellow Americans loved and trusted him. He guided the young nation's first shaky steps down the road of independence. His great skill as a leader earned him the title "Father of Our Country."

A Nation Given Grace

As the first president, George Washington served his country well. He knew that he was setting an example for every president after him. He did not make decisions quickly. He talked to the other leaders. He took time to think through problems. He tried to do what was best for everyone in the country. At the end of four years, Americans elected him to a second term. But he did not run for a third term. He decided it was better to step down and let another man be president.

The United States of America quickly took its place among the nations of the world. Many more presidents after Washington led the country through good and bad times. Today the nation has grown from thirteen states to fifty. It is a country of great wealth and power. It has been able to help many other nations of the world.

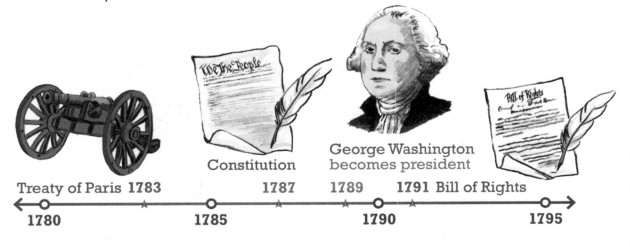

Treaty of Paris **1783**

Constitution **1787**

George Washington becomes president **1789**

1791 Bill of Rights

1780   **1785**   **1790**   **1795**

When we study the history of the United States, we can see God's grace. God blessed America with wise leaders. He allowed it to be a place where people could worship and talk of Him freely. Christians from the United States have gone to many other parts of the world with the good news of Jesus Christ.

Americans have not always done what is right. But God has shown our nation grace because He is a God of grace. We can thank Him for His goodness to our country. We can pray for our leaders. And we can ask Him to help us live as citizens who always honor Him and His laws.

In what ways has God shown America grace?

Resource Treasury

Geogloss

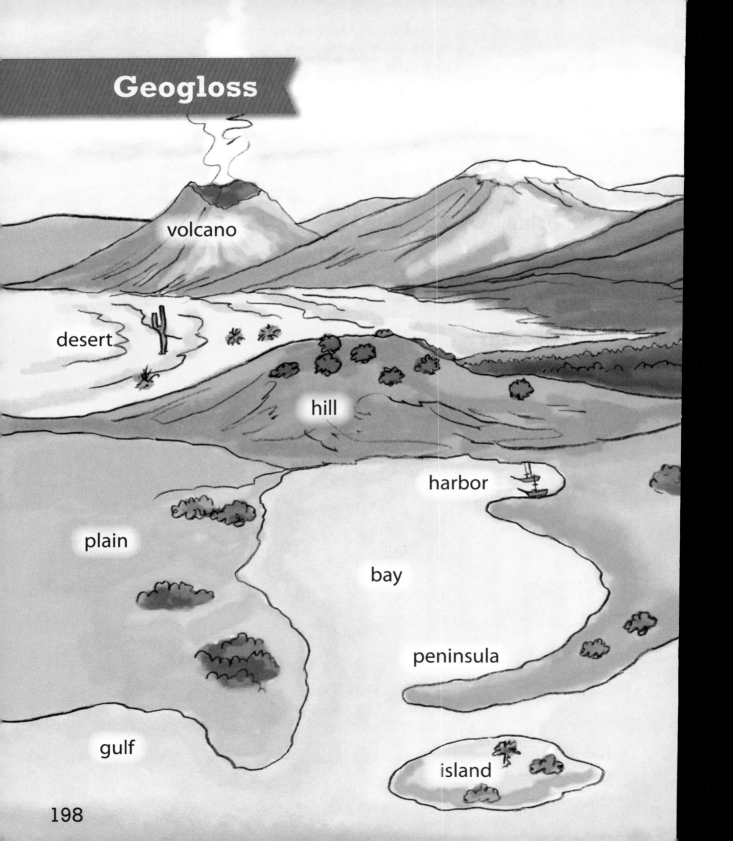

volcano

desert

hill

harbor

plain

bay

peninsula

gulf

island

mountain

cliff

valley

forest

river

lake

coast

sea

ocean

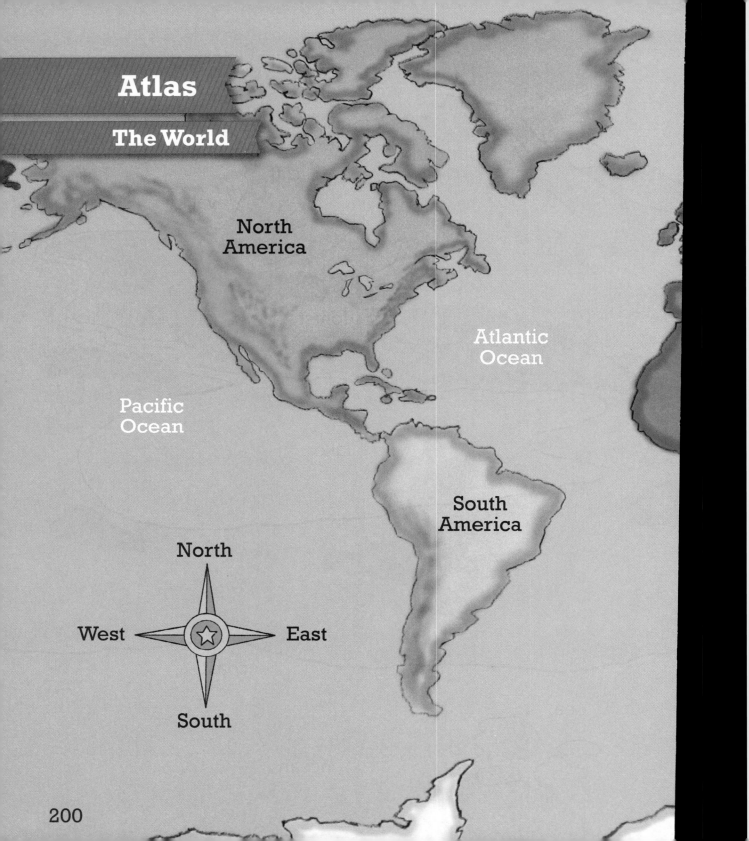

North
America

Atlantic
Ocean

Pacific
Ocean

South
America

North

West ⟵ ⭐ ⟶ East

South

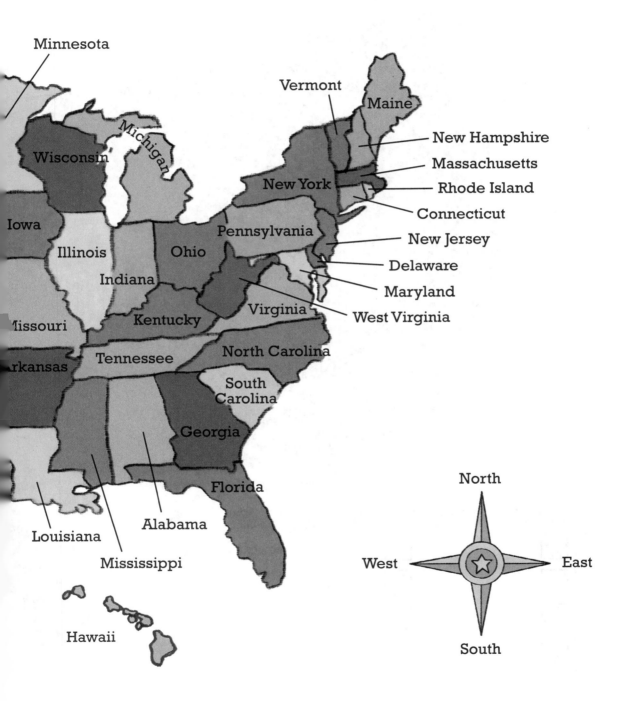

Minnesota

Wisconsin

Michigan

Iowa

Illinois

Indiana

Ohio

Missouri

Kentucky

Arkansas

Tennessee

Vermont

Maine

New Hampshire

Massachusetts

New York

Rhode Island

Connecticut

Pennsylvania

New Jersey

Delaware

Maryland

Virginia

West Virginia

North Carolina

South Carolina

Georgia

Florida

Alabama

Louisiana

Mississippi

Hawaii

North

West   East

South

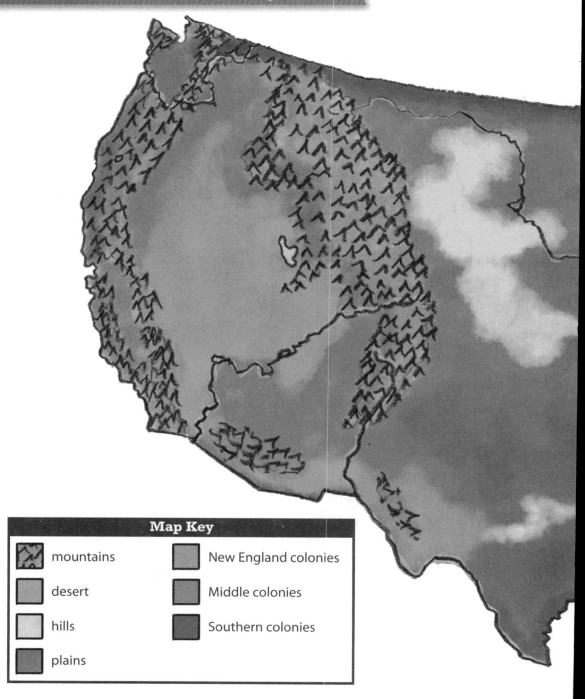

Map Key	
mountains	New England colonies
desert	Middle colonies
hills	Southern colonies
plains	

New Hampshire

New York

Massachusetts

Rhode Island

Connecticut

Pennsylvania

New Jersey

Delaware

Maryland

Virginia

North Carolina

South Carolina

Georgia

Glossary

A

adopt

to accept. *America **adopted** the Constitution in 1789.* (page 169)

ancestor

a person in your family who lived long ago. *One of my **ancestors** came to America from Germany.* (page 56)

Anglican

a person who belongs to the Church of England. *Many of the southern colonists were **Anglicans**.* (page 149)

anthem

a special song used as a symbol. *"The Star-Spangled Banner" is our national **anthem**.* (page 53)

apprentice

a boy who lived with a tradesman to learn his trade. *John became an **apprentice** to a blacksmith.* (page 127)

Articles of Confederation

America's first plan of government after the Revolutionary War. *Under the **Articles of Confederation**, the national government was not strong.* (page 181)

artifact

an object left behind by people long ago. *The museum had a large display of Iroquois **artifacts**.* (page 78)

B

ballot

a list of all the people who want to be elected. *There are five names on the **ballot** for class president.* (page 48)

bank

a safe place to keep money. *I put the money I earn in the **bank**.* (page 30)

bar graph

a chart that uses bars to compare different numbers or amounts. *The **bar graph** shows that more people in our city live in houses than in apartments.* (page 16)

Bill of Rights

a list of the people's freedoms added to the Constitution. *The **Bill of Rights** gives us freedom to speak and write about God.* (page 190)

British

citizens of England, Scotland, Ireland, and Wales in the 1700s. *The **British** traded goods with the colonies and with Africa.* (page 156)

burgess

a person elected to make laws in a colonial government. *Virginia's House of **Burgesses** was the first group of elected leaders in the colonies.* (page 135)

cash crop

an important crop depended on to make money. *Rice was a **cash crop** in the southern colonies.* (page 144)

Catholic

a person who belongs to the Roman Catholic Church. *Maryland was first settled by **Catholics**.* (page 136)

citizen

a person who belongs to a certain place. *My aunt is a **citizen** of Mexico.* (page 42)

citizenship

the study of how I can help my community, my state, and my country. *Keeping my community clean shows I have learned good **citizenship**.* (page 5)

climate

the usual weather a region has in each season. *Our **climate** has warm, dry summers and rainy winters.* (page 62)

college

a place of higher education to prepare students for their life's work. *The first American **college** was in New England.* (page 107)

colonist

a person from one country who settles in another. *The men of Jamestown were some of the first **colonists** in the New World.* (page 101)

colony

a settlement formed in one country by a group of people from another country. *A **colony** usually keeps close ties with its home country.* (page 85)

community

a place where people live and work together. *My **community** had a Fourth of July parade.* (page 24)

compass rose

a symbol that shows directions and helps us find places on a map. *The **compass rose** helps me remember that west is to the left on a map.* (page 17)

Congress

a group of lawmakers that work with the president. ***Congress** is voting on the new law this week.* (page 44)

consequence

what happens because of something we do. *A **consequence** of breaking the law might be going to jail.* (page 51)

Constitution

the plan of government written and adopted by the United States. *The **Constitution** tells what powers our government has.* (page 183)

consumer

a person who buys or uses goods. *Many **consumers** bought a new car last year.* (page 31)

continent

a big area of land. *Last year I visited the **continent** of Asia.* (page 15)

council

a group of leaders that work together in a community. *Mr. Brown has been elected to our city **council**.* (page 43)

culture

the way of life of a group of people. *I would like to study the **culture** of the Mayas.* (page 3)

dame school

a place of education for colonial children in the teacher's home. *Some children in the New England colonies attended **dame schools**.* (page 106)

debtor

a person who owes money to someone else. *Georgia was founded for **debtors** who wanted to find work.* (page 140)

Declaration of Independence

a paper in which the American colonists stated their rights and freedoms during the Revolutionary War. *The Declaration of Independence was written mostly by Thomas Jefferson.* (page 168)

declare

to make known. *The colonies needed to declare their freedom from Great Britain.* (page 168)

economics

the study of the way we use goods and money. *In our study of economics we are learning about crops farmers grow to sell.* (page 4)

education

training at home or in schools. *Many children get an education at home.* (page 106)

election

choosing leaders by voting. *Who do you think will win the election?* (page 47)

equator

the line around the widest part of a globe. *North America is north of the equator.* (page 18)

explorer

a person who travels to learn about another place. *Explorers from Europe came to North America.* (page 80)

factory

a place where people produce goods. *My father works in a factory that makes airplane parts.* (page 63)

fill

responsibility of people on earth to have children. *God wanted Adam and Eve to fill the earth.* (page 9)

freedom

a privilege that comes with responsibility. *God gave Adam and Eve freedom to eat from any tree except one.* (page 10)

French and Indian War

the war between Great Britain and France over control of North America. *The **French and Indian War** lasted seven years.* (page 157)

geography

the study of places on the earth around us. *We use maps to study the **geography** of our country.* (page 3)

globe

a ball-shaped object that shows the continents and oceans of the world. *You can see all seven continents on a **globe**.* (page 18)

goods

the things people make or sell. *We bought some **goods** at the store on the corner.* (page 31)

government

the leaders of your nation, state, and community. *God tells us to pray for those in our **government**.* (page 42)

governor

the leader of a state government. *Our **governor** plans to raise our state taxes next year.* (page 43)

grammar school

a place of education for young boys in the colonies. *The larger towns were able to pay a teacher and have a **grammar school**.* (page 107)

Great Awakening

a time in the colonies during which many people returned to God. *Jonathan Edwards was used of God as a pastor during the **Great Awakening**.* (page 111)

Great Compromise

a plan for dividing the United States government into the Senate and the House to give each state a fair number of votes. *Roger Sherman thought of the **Great Compromise**.* (page 187)

history

the study of the past. *We are learning about American **history**.* (page 2)

hornbook

a wooden paddle with a printed paper and a covering of animal horn; used by colonial children to learn to read and write. *Children sometimes carried* **hornbooks** *on a string around their necks.* (page 106)

House

the government body whose number of leaders is decided by the number of people in each state. *California has the largest number of leaders in the* **House**. (page 186)

Huguenot

a Christian in France who could not worship freely. *Some* **Huguenots** *settled in South Carolina.* (page 150)

immigrant

a person who moves to a new country. *My grandfather was an* **immigrant** *from Germany.* (page 56)

income

money earned. *I will use some of my* **income** *from weeding the garden to buy a ball glove.* (page 30)

indigo

a plant that was used to make blue dye. *Eliza Pinckney learned how to grow* **indigo**. (page 139)

judge

a leader in a court who uses laws to settle problems. *The* **judge** *decided that the man must pay a fine.* (page 51)

July 4, 1776

the date that the Declaration of Independence was adopted. *We will always remember* **July 4, 1776**, *as the beginning of our nation's freedom.* (page 169)

just

what is fair and right. *I did not think it was* **just** *for Jim to be treated better than Jon.* (page 40)

L

landform

a certain shape of land on the earth. *Hills are the most common **landform** in our area.* (page 64)

landmark

an important place or building. *The Statue of Liberty is an American **landmark**.* (page 55)

language

a way of speaking and writing within a group of people. *Peter is learning the Chinese **language**.* (page 13)

law

a rule people follow when they live together. ***Laws** help to keep a community safe.* (page 34)

longhouse

a long, narrow home built by the Iroquois. *Several families could live in a **longhouse**.* (page 77)

Loyalist

a colonist who stayed true to Great Britain. *Many **Loyalists** fought for the British during the war.* (page 163)

M

map grid

a map made up of lines that form squares. *A **map grid** helps me find places on a map.* (page 29)

massacre

the killing of many people. *Five hundred people died in the horrible **massacre**.* (page 160)

mayor

the leader of your city or town. *The **mayor** helps make laws for my community.* (page 35)

meetinghouse

a building that church was held in. *The Puritans sang the Psalms in the **meetinghouse**.* (page 105)

minuteman

a young man in the colonies trained to be ready to fight at any minute. ***Minutemen** grabbed their guns and quickly met on the green.* (page 165)

N

nation

a country. *Our **nation** celebrates its birthday on July 4.* (page 42)

natural resource

something in nature that God gives people to use. *Redwood trees are one of California's **natural resources**.* (page 61)

neighborhood

you and the people who live and work around you. *I know many of the people in my **neighborhood**.* (page 28)

North Pole

a point located at the top of a globe. *The **North Pole** stays frozen all the time.* (page 18)

O

ocean

a large body of water. *The **ocean** stretched before us as far as we could see.* (page 15)

P

Patriot

a colonist who wanted to throw off British rule. *Many **Patriots** lived in Boston in the 1770s.* (page 163)

peninsula

land with water on three sides. *Part of Florida is a **peninsula**.* (page 65)

Pilgrim

a person who did not agree with the Church of England and left it to come to America. *The **Pilgrims** sailed to America on the* Mayflower *in 1620.* (page 92)

plantation

a large farm in the South. *There are several large **plantations** in South Carolina.* (page 138)

port

a place where ships come and go. *Charleston became a busy **port** for shipping in the colonies.* (page 137)

president

the most important leader of the national government. *The **president** of the United States lives in the White House.* (page 44)

producer

a person who makes, grows, or sells goods. *Fruit growers in Florida are top producers of oranges.* (page 31)

Puritan

a person who did not agree with the Church of England but wanted to stay in it and help it change. *The Puritans came to America ten years after the Pilgrims did.* (page 96)

Q

Quaker

a religious group in England who believed people are guided by an "inner light." *Quakers were the first Europeans to settle Pennsylvania.* (page 117)

R

region

a part of a country with a certain climate or features. *The Southwest is a hot, dry region in our country.* (page 60)

religion

a person's belief about where he came from, how to worship, and how to live. *The Puritans came to America because of their religion.* (page 93)

religious freedom

liberty for people of many different religions. *People from all over Europe came to America for religious freedom.* (page 119)

republic

a kind of government in which citizens choose their leaders. *The United States of America is a republic.* (page 185)

responsibility

something that you should do. *We have a responsibility to obey our teacher.* (page 50)

revolution

people fighting to change their government. *The colonists' desire for freedom led to a revolution.* (page 166)

Revolutionary War

the war between the colonists and the British. *The Revolutionary War was fought from 1775 to 1783.* (page 166)

right

something that you are free to do. *Citizens age eighteen and older have the right to vote.* (page 46)

ruin

what is left of a building from long ago. *Mayan ruins can still be seen today in South America.* (page 79)

rule

responsibility of people on earth to care for things God made. *God told Adam and Eve to rule over the earth.* (page 9)

rural

far from a city; in "the country." *My family lives in a rural area in Iowa.* (page 27)

S

Senate

the government body with an equal number of leaders from each state. *Each state has two leaders in the Senate.* (page 186)

service

a job or a skill that helps people. *Doctors offer an important service.* (page 31)

shelter

a home. *Native Americans had many kinds of shelters.* (page 75)

slave

a person who works for someone else without pay or the hope of freedom. *Europeans brought many African slaves into the colonies to help with farming.* (page 88)

South Pole

a point located at the bottom of a globe. *The South Pole is on the continent of Antarctica.* (page 18)

suburb

a community near a city but away from the busy part. *Our home is in a suburb of Chicago.* (page 26)

surrender

to give up a fight. *The British surrendered to the Americans at the Battle of Yorktown.* (page 175)

symbol

something that reminds citizens of an important person or idea. *The bald eagle is a symbol of America's freedom and bravery.* (page 52)

tax

money used by community leaders to pay for goods and services the community needs. *The taxes we pay are used to help keep our community safe and clean.* (page 35)

term

the four-year period that the president serves. *President George Washington served two terms.* (page 191)

trade

a job that takes special skill. *My brother wants to learn the trade of shipbuilding.* (page 104)

tradition

a special way of doing something for many years. *Baking sugar cookies is one of my family's favorite Christmas traditions.* (page 130)

Treaty of Paris

the agreement that ended the Revolutionary War. *The Treaty of Paris was signed in 1783.* (page 175)

urban

in a city. *People in urban areas might live close to offices and stores.* (page 26)

volunteer

a person who does not get paid for his services. *The people who cleaned up our street after the storm were volunteers.* (page 32)

vote

the way we choose leaders. *Today our nation will vote for its next president.* (page 47)

wampum

small beads that the Iroquois made
from shells. *The Iroquois traded
wampum for English goods.* (page 77)

Index

Photograph Credits

2t Marmaduke St. John/Alamy; 2b © National Geographic/SuperStock; 3 © iStockphoto.com/BartCo; 4, 30b, 31br, 60b Getty Images/Comstock Images/Thinkstock; 5 © iStockphoto.com/Kali Nine; 6bg, 7 zothen/Bigstock.com; 6fg, 38fg, 58fg, 72fg, 90fg, 106, 112fg, 132fg, 154fg, 169, 178fg BJU Photo Services; 14t © iStockphoto.com/avdeev007; 14b © iStockphoto.com/digitalskillet; 15tl © iStockphoto.com/BDphoto; 15tr, 15br, 26l, 30cbl, 30cbr, 45l, 54c, 54r, 55l, 58bg, 59, 60t, 63l, 64t, 64c, 65b, 66t, 66c, 66b, 70, 72bg, 73, 112bg, 113, 126b, 127tl, 127tr, 140l Getty Images/iStockphoto/Thinkstock; 15bl © iStockphoto.com/THEGIFT777; 18 © iStockphoto.com/Nigel Spiers; 22bg, 23 Jupiterimages/Comstock/Thinkstock; 22fg Getty Images/Wavebreak Media/Thinkstock; 26r Jupiter Images/Brand X/Thinkstock; 27 Jupiterimages/Pixland/Thinkstock; 28, 127bl Getty Images/Hemera/Thinkstock; 30t iStockphoto/Thinkstock; 30ctl Getty Images/Thomas Northcut/Photodisc/Thinkstock; 30ctr Getty Images/Zoonar/Thinkstock; 31tl Getty Images/Nick White/Digital Vision/Thinkstock; 31tr © Design Pics/SuperStock; 31bl Getty Images/Design Pics/Thinkstock; 34 © iStockphoto.com/olaser; 35 © iStockphoto.com/YinYang; 36t Dave Kotinsky/Getty Images Entertainment/Getty Images; 36bl "Twin Towers-NYC" by Carol M. Highsmith/Wikimedia Commons/Public Domain; 36br © Alan Crosthwaite/Dreamstime.com; 37l Library of Congress; 37r "Brooklyn Bridge NYC August 16, 2010" by Webfan29/Wikimedia Commons/CC-By-SA 3.0; 38bg, 39 © iStockphoto.com/Jonathan P. Larsen; 45r © Mikael Karlsson/Alamy; 46 © Visions of America/SuperStock; 48 © David R. Frazier Photolibrary, Inc./Alamy; 49t "Official Portrait of President Reagan 1981"/White House/Wikimedia/Public Domain; 49b © Everett Collection/Alamy; 52 © iStockphoto.com/Syldavia; 54l André Nantel/Bigstock.com; 54b © Gary Blakeley/Dreamstime.com; 55r Jose Gil/Bigstock.com; 61l © iStockphoto.com/jjmm888; 61r Bob Stefko/Photographer's Choice/Getty Images; 63r Corel Corporation; 64b © iStockphoto.com/druvo; 65t Comstock/Thinkstock; 68 Jeffrey Banke/Bigstock; 69l Ron and Patty Thomas/Photographer's Choice/Getty Images; 69r © William Perry/Dreamstime.com; 71 © iStockphoto.com/Holger Mette; 77 Hiawatha Wampum Belt/Iroquois Indian Museum, Howes Cave, NY; 78l © Pat Canova/Alamy; 78r Werner Forman/Universal Images Group/Getty Images; 107 "Harvard 1740" by William Burgis/Wikimedia Commons/Public Domain; 79 Getty Images/Goodshoot RF/Thinkstock; 80 "2000Leif Ericson obv" Designed and engraved by John Mercanti/Wikimedia Commons/Public Domain; 89 "Hunt-Shrine" by Ser Amantio di Nicolao/Wikipedia Commons/CC-by-SA 3.0; 90bg, 91 Raymond Forbes/SuperStock; 104t imagebroker.net/SuperStock; 104b © iStockphoto.com/Gina Groves; 120, 121 Penn's Grid for Philadelphia/Public Domain; 126t © 2009 JupiterImages Corporation/liquidlibrary; 127br Getty Images/Ingram Publishing/Thinkstock; 132bg, 133 © Americanspirit/Dreamstime.com; 135t, 135b The Colonial Williamsburg Foundation; 135c Raymond B.